P9-AGA-244

THE NOVEL-MACHINE

The Novel-Machine
The Theory
and Fiction of Anthony Trollope

Walter M. Kendrick

The Johns Hopkins University Press
Baltimore and London

This book was brought to publication with the generous assistance of the Andrew W. Mellon Foundation.

Copyright © 1980 by The Johns Hopkins University Press

All rights reserved. No part of this book may be reproduced or transmitted in any form or by any means, electronic or mechanical, including photocopying, recording, xerography, or any information storage and retrieval system, without permission in writing from the publisher.

Manufactured in the United States of America

The Johns Hopkins University Press, Baltimore, Maryland 21218
The Johns Hopkins Press Ltd., London

Library of Congress Catalog Card Number 79-18294
ISBN 0-8018-2301-3

Library of Congress Cataloging in Publication data will be found on the last printed page of this book.

FOR OLIVE AND WALTER L. KENDRICK

It is quite true that his novels are superficial, that they deal almost entirely with costume and manner, that they do not concern themselves with psychological problems, that they studiously avoid great passions, and that they never present the poetic aspect of men and things. . . . His mind presents no very salient point, it possesses no very special characteristic. He is witty, but not supremely so; he has humour, but no one would ever dream of speaking of him as a humourist; he can laugh at the follies in our social arrangements, but he is not a satirist; he can moralize prettily enough, but he has no claim to be a teacher; he can turn a sentence or an epigram with considerable neatness, but he will never be ranked amongst the masters of style. He has his share of all intellectual and artistic qualities, but he has nothing in excess; he inherits all the powers of the great novelists, but he has no very large inheritance of any one of these powers. And it is for this reason that we cannot attach any very distinctive personality to Mr. Trollope.

—Alexander Smith, "Novels and Novelists of the Day," *North British Review*

I am realistic.
—Trollope, *An Autobiography*

CONTENTS

PREFACE

THE NOVEL-MACHINE proceeds according to the following plan: its first five short chapters rewrite the *Autobiography* as an undisguised theory of realistic fiction, exploring its paradoxes while placing it in the context of mid-Victorian criticism. Chapters 6 and 7 survey the manifestations in Trollope's novels of what his theory sets down as the primary difference of realism: its way of telling its readers how to read. Chapter 8 is a close reading of *He Knew He Was Right*, a neglected novel that deserves to stand in much higher critical esteem than it does. The reading is closer than that to which any of Trollope's novels have so far been subjected; it shows how deeply woven into the texture of his writing the rhetoric of realism is. This plan is a departure from the usual method of criticizing Trollope—surveying the whole of his work a novel at a time, saying a little about every novel and always too little about each. *He Knew He Was Right* is typical but also unique—just as all of Trollope's novels are, just as Trollope is.

I wish to thank J. Hillis Miller, Perry Meisel, and Christina Stancarone, who read the manuscript at various stages of its progress and offered helpful advice and criticism.

Preparation of the manuscript was financed in part by a grant from the Fordham University Faculty Research Council, to whom my thanks are also due.

xi

NOTE ON TEXTS

THE TEXT OF *An Autobiography* referred to throughout the following study is that of the Oxford World's Classics edition, edited by Frederick Page (London: Oxford University Press, 1953).

Because there is no standard edition of Trollope's novels, I have used a variety of editions—the volumes in the World's Classics series when these have been available, others when they have not been. References to Trollope's novels indicate chapter numbers only. I have followed the plan of continuous chapter numbering used by Winifred Gerould and James Gerould in *A Guide to Trollope* (Princeton: Princeton University Press, 1948).

For *He Knew He Was Right*, I have used the reprint of the first edition edited by P. D. Edwards (St. Lucia: University of Queensland Press, 1974).

THE NOVEL-MACHINE

INTRODUCTION

A World under Glass

THE ART OF the mid-Victorian realistic novel flourished in innocence of theory. The great realistic novelists wrote occasional essays on the fiction of others and commented occasionally on their own. Professional critics, confined mostly to anonymous periodical reviews, attempted to evaluate each new example of the realistic art according to some general understanding of what fiction is or ought to be. But no one, novelist or critic, felt it necessary to explain or justify with theory the fundamental proposition of realism—that the purpose of fiction is to represent the real world accurately and improvingly in writing. Critics might debate the accuracy of one or another fictional representation of life, and novelists might defend their work against charges of unwholesomeness or moral inefficacy, but that fiction did represent life and that the representation must have a moral effect on its reader were coupled assumptions that no one sought to dispute. Critics and novelists alike accepted realism as natural and necessary; when they theorized, which was seldom, they took the realistic proposition as their starting point and went confidently on from there.

For Henry James, most prominent spokesman for the next generation of English novelists and critics, this neglect of theory was the greatest sin

of all his predecessors. Even George Eliot, the most theoretical of mid-
Victorian realists, was guilty of it: she theorized about life more than art,
and about art in general much more than about her own. The worst
sinner of all was Anthony Trollope, the least theoretical of realists, who
apparently theorized about nothing at all. "As an artist," James wrote of
the recently deceased Trollope in 1883, "he never took himself seriously."
This was, according to James, Trollope's response to "a certain English
ideal"—that it is "rather dangerous to be explicitly or consciously an
artist—to have a system, a doctrine, a form." Trollope had "as little form
as possible"; he "never troubled his head nor clogged his pen with theories
about the nature of his business."[1]

Trollope's neglect of theory led to his denigration by James and other
self-conscious artists of the late nineteenth century. The same deficiency
has also influenced his evaluation by twentieth-century critics. As Ruth
apRoberts observes, Trollope has been particularly subject to both dismissal and belletristic "appreciation" because his art escapes from the
categories of the traditional critical vocabulary.[2] Not only does Trollope
lack theory and form, but he is also short on unity, structure, style, point
of view, and all the other things that have made fiction susceptible to
criticism. Trollope has traditionally led his critics into what David Skilton
calls the fallacy of the transparent or disappearing novel[3]—the implicit
assumption that the featurelessness of Trollope's writing allows one to
treat his represented world as if it were not represented but real, as if the
texts that constitute that world were made of glass, or else not there at all.

Perhaps because they are as firmly devoted to the realistic proposition
as their Victorian predecessors were, Trollope's twentieth-century critics,
even the most recent of them,[4] have failed to observe that textual transparency is as much a theoretical matter as a practical one. To read
Trollope's texts as if they were windows on the real world is probably
the easiest thing to do with them; it seems now, as much as it did a
century ago, the "natural" way to read any texts that claim only to
represent reality. Yet to accept such a way of reading means to accept
as well a certain relation between writing and reading, reading and

[1]"Anthony Trollope: A Partial Portrait," *Century*, n. s. 4 (July 1883): 385-95; reprinted
in Donald Smalley, ed., *Trollope: The Critical Heritage* (London: Routledge & Kegan Paul,
1969), pp. 526-27.
[2]*Trollope: Artist and Moralist* (London: Chatto & Windus, 1971), chap. 1.
[3]*Anthony Trollope and His Contemporaries: A Study in the Theories and Conventions
of Mid-Victorian Fiction* (London: Longmans, 1972), p. 138.
[4]This is true of even the best recent study of Trollope, James R. Kincaid's *The Novels of
Anthony Trollope* (Oxford: Clarendon Press, 1977).

living, fiction and what is not fictional. It means to agree upon implicit definitions of all these terms and their values. It means to assent, consciously or not, to an entire system of discourse that follows from the realistic proposition and serves it. This system of discourse, this theory, is implicit in all realistic fiction, and in all criticism and reading that take the realistic way as natural.

That no one ever wrote this theory down as such would not hinder its existence or its efficacy. The theory would remain in effect every time a novel made a statement about a fictional world and every time a critic or reader took that statement as meaning something real. It would continue to govern the work of any critic who wrote about plot, character, scene, development, or any other term in the traditional critical vocabulary that, in the twentieth century as well as the nineteenth, has restricted what criticism can see by dictating what it is able to say. In fact, however, the theory was written down as such, at a time when its universal acceptance as natural made the explicit statement of it look like the banal assertion of clichés. For Trollope's traditional critics, his *Autobiography* has remained as banal as it was when it was published in 1883. But for the present study, which attempts to get outside the shared enclosure of realism and what has traditionally been said about it, this cliché-ridden book is the clearest, most comprehensive statement of the theory of realism that realism itself has ever produced.

Trollope's *Autobiography* does not look like a book of theory, and none of Trollope's traditional critics has taken it for one. It looks like the story of Trollope's life, heavily interspersed with comments about his art. It has been the principal source for Trollope's biographers; what it says about his life is commonplace enough, and it also seems to be true. What it says about his art is confined mostly to the description of how he wrote his books and how he expected them to be read. This seems to be true as well, and it is so extremely commonplace that it becomes amazing. The *Autobiography* was mainly responsible for the sharp decline in Trollope's reputation that set in after his death. To James and the other artistic novelists of the late nineteenth century, it looked like the confessions of an unabashed hack, who ground out fiction by the shelf-full and bragged obnoxiously about how much money he made from it. The unreflective, mechanical system described in the *Autobiography* would seem to preclude theory altogether, since the Trollopian novelist never slows down long enough to take a look at what he has been doing, let alone to theorize about it.

Indeed, the *Autobiography* specifically warns the would-be realistic novelist not to slow down. In an analogy that James and his successors have found particularly outrageous, Trollope compares the realistic writer to a shoemaker. Any venture into reflexiveness is forbidden him if he would be realistic: he is at his best when he writes as quickly as possible, without notes, without a rough draft, without even thinking about what he is going to write until he writes it. This is the only way of writing realistically; Trollope himself has written this way, and he advises any aspiring realist to follow him. What the *Autobiography* describes is not an artist, not even anything so human as a shoemaker. The realistic novelist, according to Trollope, is a machine for the production of novels. The *Autobiography* declares in its first sentence that it has that title only "for the want of a better name." The title of the present study, *The Novel-Machine*, is my version of that better name.

The realistic novel, for Trollope, is never a static structure to be contemplated or reflected upon. It is always dynamic, a process rather than an object. It exists only as the nonstop sequence of conception, writing, selling, and reading; at no point in the sequence should anyone's attention double back upon itself. The stillness of esthetic contemplation, which for the Jamesian-Paterian critics of the late nineteenth century and after is the aim and value of all art, does not exist for Trollopian realism. This absence, indeed, is probably the reason why the *Autobiography* has never been recognized as a theoretical work. It is a theory not of the novel but of novel production, and a criticism whose paradigm is the lyric poem, a self-contained linguistic object, has not been able to see that it is a theory at all.

It is clear from the numerous and severe regulations that the *Autobiography* imposes on the realistic writer that, for Trollope, there is nothing "natural" about textual transparency. Rather, it is a goal to be achieved, and considerable labor is required in achieving it. Writing is not transparent by nature, but it can be made so under the proper treatment: the art of realism consists in forcing writing to efface itself between the equal realities of the reader's real and the writer's represented world. The fundamental difference between the realist and all other dealers in writing—whether they be poets, sensationalists, or the writers of any rough draft—is that the realist has thoroughly tamed his medium, while the others have all, to some degree, surrendered to it. The taming of his medium is the primary enterprise of the realistic novelist, and when it is accomplished it is the primary sign by which realistic writing can be recognized. That sign is a difference and an absence: realistic writing can be recognized because it is different from all other kinds, and the difference consists in the absence from realistic writing of all the marks of self-indulgence that characterize other writing. Realistic writing is dependent upon its opposite: not only is textual transparency, for Trollope, not the "natural" state of things, but it presupposes the fact that there are other ways to write.

Life, for the realist, is always said to come first, and writing follows. In the description of his own writing practice, Trollope locates all his art and all his pleasure in a time before any writing is done, while writing itself is pure mechanical drudgery. This is also his standard for ranking the novelists of his day: the negative mark of realism, which distinguishes the realistic text from all others, is also the evidence that its writer has "lived with" his characters before he writes them down. The more thoroughly he keeps life and writing separate, giving the one total precedence over the other, the better realist he is. The fecundity of the real world stands in a relation of permanent priority and excess to the writing that attempts to represent it, but there is no danger, only joy, in the fullness of reality. Rather, as the present study will demonstrate in its first four chapters, the danger is that writing will seek its own infinitude, coming detached from its bondage to the real in a vain effort to catch up with everything that is. Even worse, writing threatens always to double back upon itself, making itself its own subject and opening up a labyrinth of metalanguage into which it is the death of realism to stray. When writing is published and read, it becomes as real as the world in which it circulates and which it represents; but writing would supplant that world if it had the chance. Reality must be enforced upon writing as its limit; textual transparency is neither the natural nor the original state of things, though it claims, for its own sake, to be both. The desire to produce a text, as Trollope's theory of realism covertly admits, precedes even for the realist the desire to have a subject.

This is not a new admission with Trollope; writers have always admitted it. What is new with Trollope is only the written anxiety that writing will pervert its own nature unless it is kept under constant surveillance. This anxiety is native to fictional realism, its original neurosis. Writing has always been recognized as prior to the representation of reality, and sometimes even to reality itself; but since Trollope the recognition has been accompanied by a special guilt, the embarrassed and censorious confession that, in E. M. Forster's words, "the pen always finds life difficult to record; left to itself, it records the pen."[5] That this is a

---

[5] "Sanditon" (1925), reprinted in *Abinger Harvest* (New York: Harcourt, Brace & World, 1936), p. 153.

sin, as Jacques Derrida has amply shown, has been a major tenet of Western metaphysics since Plato at least; but it is in the theory of fictional realism, most conscientiously laid down in Trollope's *Autobiography*, that the original sin of writing obtains its most extreme definition and its fullest penance.

Writing, for Trollope, is never glamorous or even interesting. It is a mechanical matter of placing one's haunches in a chair and taking hold of a pen, with the object of peddling what comes of it. The product of this activity is there to be measured, parceled out, and bent to a purpose. It has no value in itself, and the only value it can ever assume is that of complete transparency. It is the sole purpose of realistic writing to recreate in the reader's mind exactly the condition that existed in the novelist's before he sat down to write. Writing done realistically becomes pure conveyance, a medium without a message, an absolutely lucid glass. Realistic writing, for Trollope, does not represent; it transmits. The paradox is, however, that when writing disappears and only two equal minds remain, there can be no representation, no signification—in fact, no transmission. This is, of course, the impasse of realism, not its project. It is the hyperbolic vanishing point toward which realism strives but which, if it were ever attained, would mean the end of realism. The project of realism is to use writing against itself, to make it disappear between two equivalent realities; but the project also depends on the conservation of the difference between writing and reality, a difference that is conserved by the same gesture that seeks to efface writing. Reality is defined in writing, and its definition is that it is different from what defines it. No matter how far toward disappearance writing might be pushed, it must not disappear utterly, or else the real world too would vanish.

Realistic writing, for Trollope, is absolutely literal, not metaphoric. But when he comes in the *Autobiography* to describe the project of realism as a whole, he finds that nothing will do so well as a metaphor. The figure, however, is not Trollope's own; it is Hawthorne's, the poetical product of a writer whose work is "the very opposite" of Trollope's (124). Hawthorne wrote in 1860 that Trollope's novels are "just as real as if some giant had hewn a great lump out of the earth and put it under a glass case, with all its inhabitants going about their business, and not suspecting that they were being made a show of" (125). This, comments Trollope, "describes with wonderful accuracy the purport that I have ever had in view in my writing." What it describes has nothing to do with how novels are written and little with what they convey. Rather, it describes how a realistic novel ought to be regarded by its reader if it is to be realistic.

There is no novelist in the business: the giant is nowhere to be seen, and the only trace of his former presence is the enclosure he has made. That enclosure is designed to be looked through, not at: the novel's textuality, the fact that it is writing, makes the novel possible but ought to be ignored. The only difference between the world inside and the world outside is the glass. Without it, there would be a flawless continuity from the enclosed world to the world where the reader stands, but in that case there would be no novel. With it, there can be no realism unless the reader simultaneously sees the glass and pretends that he does not see it. The metonymic enterprise of realism, which Roman Jakobson (following Trollope or at least echoing him) opposes to the metaphoric enterprise of Romantic and Symbolist poetry,[6] is portrayed in this figure as a paradox: there can be a metonymic relation between the enclosed world and the outside world only when the enclosure is acknowledged; but the enclosure, by imposing a space, however thin, between the two, prevents the relation from being anything but metaphoric. The realistic novel, far from being the transparent transcription of life, is a metarhetorical trick—a metaphor disguised, as in Trollope's borrowed figure, as metonymy.

The realistic novel, as Trollope describes it, is a thoroughly rhetorical, not representational, work of art. Even taken at its word, realism promises only to be an assignment of values and relations to a world that preexists it. This, like the art of the preacher and the politician, is a rhetorical enterprise. Taken at somewhat more than its word, realism is a rhetorical discourse committed to the endless repetition of the assertion that it is not rhetorical. Beyond a certain cultural faith on which the realistic writer can depend without mentioning it, there is nothing to tell a reader what to do with realism except realism itself. That reality is prior and superior to writing, that writing is at its best when it disappears, that looking through glass texts is the natural way to read—realistic texts themselves have been the principle conveyors of these lessons. No kind of writing has ever taken greater pains to preach how it ought to be read than the realistic kind.

Carried along by their shared acceptance of the realistic proposition, Trollope's critics have been unable to observe the operation and effects of this constitutive rhetoric of reality. The rhetoric is visible to some degree

[6]"Two Aspects of Language and Two Types of Aphasic Disturbances," in Roman Jakobson and Morris Halle, *Fundamentals of Language*, 2nd ed. (The Hague: Mouton, 1971), p. 92.

in all realistic novels, but nowhere is it more prominent than in the novels of Trollope, who gave realism its theory and its most thorough enactment. Trollope's novels are so permeated by it that they are, as his theory too would make them, manuals of realistic reading at least as much as stories about the real world. As much as they write about life, Trollope's novels write about themselves, teaching their readers how to live but also teaching them how to read. The magnitude of the task is reflected in the magnitude of Trollope's oeuvre, a vast outpouring of stories that exceeded by a few volumes the life of the man who wrote them. It may be that the vastness of the real world, escaping always beyond the reach of writing, drives the realist to extremes in the effort to record it. But it may also be that the vastness of writing compels its own extremity, and that readers need constant instruction on how to read in such an unnatural way as the realistic one.

The Death
of Anthony Trollope

NO WRITER BEGINS his autobiography more modestly than Trollope, or more strategically:

> In writing these pages, which, for the want of a better name, I shall be fain to call the autobiography of so insignificant a person as myself, it will not be so much my intention to speak of the little details of my private life, as of what I, and perhaps other round me, have done in literature; of my failures and successes such as they have been, and their causes; and of the opening which a literary career offers to men and women for the earning of their bread. And yet the garrulity of old age, and the aptitude of a man's mind to recur to the passages of his own life, will, I know, tempt me to say someting of myself;—nor, without doing so, should I know how to throw my matter into any recognised and intelligible form. That I, or any man, should tell everything of himself, I hold to be impossible. (1)

Though the modesty may be sincere, it is also strategic, and *An Autobiography* has never been given full credit for the guile with which it manages its sincerity. From its deceptively straightforward opening sentences until its close, *An Autobiography* is a tour de force in the difficult rhetorical art that Trollope made his own—the effacement of rhetoric.

That the subject of an autobiography ought to be the writer himself is announced by the title: self-life-writing. It is becomingly (or embar-

rassingly) modest for a writer to declare, in the first sentence of his autobiography, that he is "insignificant" and that only senile convenience will
"tempt me to say something of myself." This display of modesty, however,
earns a rhetorical benefit that outweighs whatever might be lost from the
reader's respect for a man who begins his life story with an apology. The
separation of Trollope's life from what he has "done in literature" divides
him in two, a division that will be multiplied as *An Autobiography* goes
on. The two subjects are of unequal value: Trollope's "intention" is to
speak generally about literature as a profession and what he has done in
it; to speak about himself is to treat what is "insignificant," though there
is an appeal to insignificance that may cause that intention to swerve. To
some degree, the swerve is also necessary: self-writing is a temptation to
tell lies, but it gives the book its "recognised and intelligible form." If the
temptation were not yielded to sometimes, the valuable part of the
undertaking would be lost in strangeness and obscurity. This structure of
unequal but interdependent opposition, where value requires the service
of that which has no value, will govern the theory of literature that *An
Autobiography* expounds. For all its modesty, the first paragraph of *An
Autobiography* accomplishes a good deal in a strategic way. It sets up the
rhetorical structures that will organize the rest of the book, it propounds
an economy of value and investment that will later be said to prevail in
all aspects of novel making, and it subtracts two-thirds of what the
book's title seemed to give. With self and life set aside as insignificant, all
that remains is writing.

In its early chapters, the *Autobiography* seems to contradict the
assurances of its first page. Until chapter 4, when the novels begin, the
narrative follows the order of Trollope's life and is apparently about
nothing else. The autobiographer also goes far toward telling "everything
about himself," a feat that is declared impossible on page 1. Amid the
more-than-Dickensian squalor of his childhood, Trollope suffers extrava-
gantly. His family is always in an uproar, moving from house to house,
often with the bailiffs close behind. His father, possessing "a certain
aptitude to do things differently from others" (2), manages to squander
all his money, insult all his friends, and waste the last years of his life on
the hopeless project of an *Ecclesiastical Encyclopedia*, a sort of Christian
key to all mythologies, which ends "buried in the midst of that huge pile
of futile literature, the building up of which has broken so many hearts"
(12). Trollope's mother, more resourceful though just as impractical,
embarks on a series of unlikely schemes to remake the family fortune,

culminating in a bazaar in Cincinnati. But everything fails until, more or less inadvertently, she writes *Domestic Manners of the Americans*, propelling herself into a career of considerable fame and, according to her son's tally, 114 volumes (28). Even this success, however, is darkened by its circumstances: "to nurse three dying patients—the patients being her husband and children—and to write novels for the sustenance of the family! It was about this period of her career that her best novels were written" (26).

Melancholy scenes like this will never be found in the novels that Anthony will grow up to write. Indeed, the story of Trollope's childhood is so extremely melancholy that it threatens to turn funny—a threat that is not at all relieved by the detached, ironic tone of the narrator, who finds even in the family's disastrous flight from Harrow "a scene of devastation" that "still was not without its amusement" (22-23). Trollope admits to having narrated such scenes "almost as coldly as I have often done some scene of intended pathos in fiction" (29). One reason for the coldness, as he acknowledges, is that forty years have passed between the living of the scenes and their narration. Another reason—though he does not acknowledge this—is that the sufferings of Anthony Trollope have little directly to do with such scenes. Rather, he suffers because he is excluded from all scenes of community, melancholy or otherwise.

The autobiographer's indignation—and there is a good deal of it—is directed entirely at his ostracism from the society of the schools he attends. None is directed at his family, though every member of it goes to America without Anthony, leaving behind no provision for his money, his transportation, least of all, his amusement. The vehemence of his complaints about his treatment at Winchester and Harrow—"I became a Pariah . . . I suffered horribly! . . . The indignities I endured are not to be described" (8-10)—suggests that Harrow is at least a partial substitute for Harrow Weald. Anthony's schoolfellows exclude him cruelly, but they do so because his family has thrown him into a society for which he is unsuited and unprepared. His family has thrown him there because it is preoccupied with itself, excluding him as cruelly as his schoolfellows do. Trollope's family and schooling have the same effect on him: driven outside the living circles of family and school, he is primed for the next substitution—novels for life.

The *Autobiography* specifies no date of origin for Trollope's habit of making fiction. At fifteen he takes up the "dangerous habit of keeping a journal," but he drops the habit after ten years and destroys the journal, "with many blushes," in 1870 (36).[1] Coexisting with the journal, and surviving it by far, is the habit of "castle building." This habit begins "six or seven years before I went to the Post Office" in 1834 (37), which would place its origin in 1827 or 1828, about the time Trollope's mother sets out for America, where she begins her literary career. Journal keeping and castle building coexist for a few years, but the former stops and its record is eventually destroyed. The latter continues and comes to no such definite end; it merges with the habit of novel building, which remains with Trollope to the end of his life.

Both habits contribute to the eventual writing of novels. Journal keeping trains Trollope in "the rapid use of pen and ink" and teaches him how to express himself "with facility" (36). Castle building has a more significant effect: "I have often doubted whether, had it not been my practice, I should ever have written a novel. I learned in this way to maintain an interest in a fictitious story, to dwell on a work created by my own imagination, and to live in a world altogether outside the world of my own material life" (37). Both habits are reflexive. The journal keeper writes a record of his life that he alone may read; the castle builder imagines a story that only he can follow. It might seem that keeping a journal is a more mature and productive habit than building castles in the air, and that the latter habit should develop naturally into the former, as reality replaces fantasy in the maturing mind. For Trollope, however, journal keeping is a youthful detour, while castle building leads directly to a grown-up profession. It is the real-life stories, not the fantasies, that maturity destroys.

The mature novelist is not born from the young man who tries to write his own life down. He derives not from the writer but from the dreamer, the builder of castles that do not copy real life but replace it: "As a boy, even as a child, I was thrown much upon myself. I have explained, when speaking of my schooldays, how it came to pass that other boys would not play with me. I was therefore alone, and had to form my plays within myself. . . . Thus it came to pass that I was always going about with some castle in the air firmly built within my mind" (36). In these daydreams, life is better than real. The dreamer is a "hero"; he is "a very clever person, and beautiful young women used to be fond of me." The dreamer is also almost a novelist. Trollope's mature practice is

---

[1]In real life, Trollope also kept a commonplace book, which he did not destroy. It is discussed by N. John Hall in "Trollope's Commonplace Book, 1835-40," *Nineteenth-Century Fiction* 31 (1976): 15-25.

"the same" as his youthful dreaming—"with this difference, that I have discarded the hero of my early dreams, and have been able to lay my own identity aside" (37).

In Trollope's novels, castle building is an unproductive habit, indulged in by young people whose desires exceed their prospects and who therefore take refuge in imagination. Johnny Eames habitually builds "those pernicious castles in the air" (*The Small House at Allington*, 10), and at one point in the same novel Adolphus Crosbie constructs "a floating castle in the air, rather than the image of a thing that might by possibility be realised" (35). Trollope's fictional castle builders always outgrow the habit; their fantasies are replaced by recognition of what is real. Johnny Eames resigns himself to bacherlorhood (*The Last Chronicle of Barset*, 84), and Crosbie's high ambitions degenerate into a sordid scramble after money (44). For Trollope's characters, castle building is an immature response to a reality that is felt to be deficient, and dreaming is given up when the deficiency is either filled by something real or acknowledged as permanent. Only in the young Trollope's case do fantasy and reality establish a continuing interrelationship, and only in his case does the castle builder grow up to be a novelist.

The difference between journal keeping and castle building is the same as that between life and literature, as the *Autobiography* defines it in its first paragraph. The same unequal values also attach to the two activities. To write about one's life, at any age and in any form, is "insignificant," while to build daydreams or novels is the "proper matter" of both Trollope's life and his autobiography. Journal keeping and castle building begin in reflexiveness: young Trollope is the subject of one and the "hero" of the other. The written record of his life is irremediably centered on himself, and though he does not destroy it for many years, it leads to nothing and eventually becomes an embarrassment to its writer. This, too, is the status of the "little details" of Trollope's life in the *Autobiography*. To record at least some of them is apparently necessary, as the journal was, but they are of no importance and require an apology. The advantage to castle building is that it can be decentered; the heroic dreamer can step out of his dreams, and yet he can go on dreaming. The change is aided by the fact that the castles are not written down, and so no permanent record of his follies remains to convict their builder. The decentering of his dreams, his own removal from the center to a place outside, turns the dreamer into a novelist. It is this change, and not the decision to write his dreams down, that brings the novelist into being.

Trollope's early life, as the *Autobiography* tells it, differs in one important respect from the careers of the youthful castle builders in his fiction. For them, as for Johnny Eames, castle building is an immature compensation, and dreaming stops when the real world is accepted and joined. If Trollope had followed this path, eventually he would have grown up to take his proper place in the community for which dreams once served as a substitute. For Trollope, however, the written journal is immature, not the dreams, and maturity comes not when the dreamer joins the real world but when he commits himself to the lifelong mainte-nance of a dream world to which he has ceased to belong. When the real world pushes him out, he dreams a substitute with himself at the center; when he becomes a novelist, the same exclusion happens—only this time he excludes himself. Both the unhappy child and the successful novelist stand on the outside looking in, but the novelist is now in full control of what the child once yearned to enter: a world with no Anthony Trollope in it. For Trollope's characters, adulthood begins when air castles end, but for Trollope himself that moment is a kind of suicide, his self-willed departure from a world that continues without him. There is, however, a life after death: it is the life of a narrator.

The narrator of the *Autobiography* makes explicit this relation between himself and what he writes. The book was posthumously pub-lished and meant to be so; it is Trollope's message "from the further shore" (316). Trollope finished the *Autobiography* in April 1876, more than six years before his real death, and he made some additions to it thereafter, attaching a few footnotes and extending the table of monetary "results" as far as the £1800 he received for *John Caldigate* in 1879.[2] But the book was ready to be published at any time; the contingency of real death had no control over it. In 1871, when Trollope set out for Australia, he had left behind three finished novels, so that if the *Great Britain* sank "there would be new novels ready to come out under my name for some years to come" (297). *An Autobiography* joined *An Old Man's Love* as a similar provision against departure for death's further shore. The end of Trollope's life would not mean the end of his writing; fiction and auto-biography would share in keeping the narrator alive, though the man was dead.

To write as if one were dead might be only a tactic guaranteeing detachment, but Trollope makes more of it than this. Posthumous writing

[2]The page heading "Results" was supplied by Trollope's son Henry, to whom the "results" of *An Autobiography* were bequeathed. The term is characteristic, however; Henry probably borrowed it from his father.

sets him free to "say what no one now does dare to say in print" (34), but he uses this freedom sparingly, withholding, for example, the names of the "lily-livered curs" who slander him at school (5). Revenge on the living is not his purpose. Rather, the main advantage to being dead is that he can speak "with that absence of self-personality which the dead may claim" (191). "Self-personality" is an apparently redundant term, unrecognized by dictionaries. As Trollope uses (or coins) it here, it seems to mean self-consciousness, the awareness of oneself as a subject—and also, perhaps, as the subject of an auto-biography. Regarding the world of the living, the dead writer has made the same transition the young Trollope makes in moving from daydreams to novels. The death of the auto-biographer allows him to write *An Autobiography*, and the same sort of rhetorical death—the willed removal of the narrator from what he narrates—turns the castle builder into the novelist.

The *Autobiography* declares emphatically that it is Trollope's novels that have enabled him to live a happy and comfortable real life. By the early 1860s, he is living "exactly the life which my thoughts and aspirations had marked out" (144). He never devotes himself entirely to novel writing, but "my hope to rise had always been built on writing novels, and at last by the writing of novels I had risen" (145). Much has been said, usually in deprecation, of the callous way in which the *Autobiography* treats fiction as a commodity, a marketable article that can be exchanged for so many pounds and so much fellowship. It has not been noted, however, that by his own account the selling of his castles in the air is the only way Trollope can give himself a real life. Reality never takes the place of fantasy, as it does for Johnny Eames. Rather, a middle term of writing is interposed. Written down as novels, Trollope's fantasies can be translated into money or friends, yet neither the world of the novels nor the world of Trollope's life is compromised by the medium that links them. The fictional world is independent and self-sustaining, but the written record of it (not the world itself) performs for Trollope a feat that only unmediated reality can perform within the fictional world —the integration of the castle builder into the community for which castles in the air were once a substitute.

The early chapters of the *Autobiography* have little explicitly to do with what Trollope has "done in literature," but, like the first chapters of many of his novels, they introduce the strategies that will govern the working out of the book's real "intention." In this case, the strategies are economic. Trollope takes up castle building to fill the manifest deficiencies in his real life; by the removal of his identity from his dreams, he becomes ready to turn the dreams into novels; and by writing down the dreams and selling them, he almost fills the deficiencies that drove him to dream in the first place—"almost," because the detour of writing has made life dependent on compensation. The dreams that began as substitutes for real life have become necessary to real life; only dreams can finance the life that started dreaming when reality fell short. This is the same kind of permanent disequilibrium that prevails between life and literature, according to the first sentences of the *Autobiography*, and a similar mechanism controls the novel-making process that the rest of the book will describe. The early chapters of the *Autobiography* bring to birth a machine for the production of novels. It is a machine driven by its own eccentricity, constantly striving to compensate for a lack that is made permanent by the very thing that ought to fill it. It is a dream-machine first of all, but when the dreams are written down they are called novels.

Character
and Conveyance

I HAVE LEFT the narrative of Trollope's life at the point where it divides in two. He has not yet begun to write novels, but he has described the decisive moment when the fantasies of a lonely child are transformed into the fictions of an adult. From this point until the end of the *Autobiography*, two narratives alternate. One treats the events in the real life of Anthony Trollope, while the other describes his methods of composition and writing, along with his opinions on novel making as an art. The one narrative is chronological and matter of fact. The other narrative interrupts the story of Trollope's life as a series of digressions ranging in length from one sentence to three chapters. The relation between the two narratives seems to be casual: something in Trollope's life will remind him of something in his art, and he will digress into art for a while, eventually returning to life. In the case of the longest digression, chapters 12 through 14, there is no obvious reason why life should be interrupted so drastically at just this point. Life merely stops at the end of chapter 11 and resumes without a gap at the start of chapter 15. The *Autobiography* has all the sloppiness of organization for which Trollope's novels have often been criticized. Indeed, it is organized much like one of those novels — an alternating pair of narratives that succeed each other in no significant order and that have little effect on each other.

The narrative of Trollope's life provides a framework for the narrative of what he has "done in literature," but that framework is both an impediment and a temptation. Life is only a vehicle. It is useful for conveying the real matter of the book, but it would be a mistake for either the writer or the reader to regard the vehicle as worthwhile in itself. Later in the *Autobiography*, a similar function and a similar low value will be attributed to plot in novels. Trollope readily admits, even insists on, the weakness of most of his plots. Yet one cannot write a novel without "a vehicle of some sort" (109), any more than one can write an autobiography without a life. Both should be ignored as much as possible: plot is "the most insignificant part of a tale" (109), and Anthony Trollope is an "insignificant" person (1).

This sort of apologetic, makeshift compromise is struck frequently in Trollope's theory. Novels and autobiography both contain elements that must be there but that are insignificant and need to be excused. For a writer who seems to control his craft as thoroughly as Trollope does, this recalcitrance in the medium is curious. The *Autobiography* speaks of plot in novels and the "little details" of Trollope's life as if they were of no interest to anybody, even the man who writes them both; yet it also allows for an unexplained attraction to them that must be resisted. Weakness may "tempt" the autobiographer to talk about himself, and the case of *Doctor Thorne* has proven that, in a novel, plot "will most raise it or most condemn it in the public judgment" (109). The public's interest in plot is ascribed to mere perversity, while the autobiographer's lapses into self-narration are excused as an old man's shortcomings. But similar restraint ought to apply on both sides of the reader-writer relation; constant effort is required to resist the lure of insignificance.

The sloppy organization of the *Autobiography* allows Trollope to detach his art from the events of his life. The origin of his art, the moment of transition from castles in the air to novels, is separated in the telling of it from the event in Trollope's life with which it might otherwise be supposed to coincide. The transition is described in a digression from the narrative of Trollope's life as he is about to enter the Civil Service in 1834. When, in 1843, he sees the ruined country house that prompts him to write *The Macdermots of Ballycloran*, the writing is easy because he is already a novelist: "When my friend left me, I set to work and wrote the first chapter or two. Up to this time, I had continued that practice of castle-building of which I have spoken; but now the castle I built was among the ruins of that old house" (60). This is the origin of writing, but it is not the origin of the novelist. The difference between daydreaming and novel making is the subtraction of the hero from the latter, and that has been done already. Writing does not make novels; all it does is write them down.

Once they are written, novels are real-life objects that function in their producer's life as any other salable commodity might do. Trollope is always very specific about when and where he does his writing, how he publishes what he writes, and how much he gets for it. It is a major cause of the decline in Trollope's reputation after the *Autobiography* was published that the book consistently treats writing as merely a physical activity, a matter of placing one's haunches in a chair and taking hold of a pen. Trollope always places writing in the "plot" of the *Autobiography*, its insignificant part. Like the selling of novels, however, writing them is distinct from the conception of the fiction. Castles in the air become novels not through writing but by laying aside the identity of the dreamer. Writing always comes later, and the novel is complete before any writing is done.

In contrast to Trollope's precision about writing and marketing his novels, he is always vague about their conception. In very few cases does the *Autobiography* indicate when or how the process of conception begins. Even in those cases, the moment of origin is vague. The "plot" of *The Macdermots of Ballycloran* is "fabricated" while Trollope is "still among the ruined walls and decayed beams" of the country house (60), and the "story" of *The Warden* is "conceived" near Salisbury Cathedral, "whilst wandering there on a mid-summer evening" (80). Plot, however, is the least important part of a novel. Far more important than plot is character, and in only a single case does the *Autobiography* describe how a character is conceived:

> My archdeacon, who has been said to be life-like, and for whom I confess that I have all a parent's fond affection, was, I think, the simple result of an effort of my moral consciousness. It was such as that, in my opinion, that an archdeacon should be,—or, at any rate, would be with such advantages as an archdeacon might have; and lo! an archdeacon was produced, who has been declared by competent authorities to be a real archdeacon down to the very ground. And yet, as far as I can remember, I had not then ever spoken to an archdeacon. I have felt the compliment to be very great. (80)

There could hardly be a greater compliment. Without drawing on any reality—without imitating anything—Trollope's moral consciousness has produced a character who is identical to life. Archdeacon Grantly's

conception has all the abruptness of a magic trick, and even a melo-
dramatic "lo!" to announce it. Indeed, it is magical, if magic means the
arrival of an effect with no visible cause.

It is hardly in keeping with Trollope's reputation, or with the
mundane tone of the *Autobiography*, to say that he produces his characters by magic. Yet this is an appropriate way of describing the sudden
equivalence of imagination and reality, when no mediate term connects
the two. Trollope has not assembled his archdeacon, nor has he imitated
a real counterpart. The *Autobiography* is careful to deny that art has
copied reality: the fictional and the real, each following its own path,
have coincided at a point, and that point is the archdeacon's birthplace.
Trollope does acknowledge that the production of novels requires observation of the world; a man is suited to be a novelist when, wherever he
goes, he is "drawing in matter from all that he has seen and heard" (198).
And certain of Trollope's own characters are admittedly copied from life,
like Sir Gregory Hardlines in *The Three Clerks*, who "was intended for"
Sir Charles Trevelyan (96). But Trollope's theory is primarily one of
production, not imitation. If the novelist copies reality, he does so only in
the general sense of possibility and probability: what an archdeacon
"should be" or "would be" is his standard, not what any real archdeacon
is.

This kind of structure recurs frequently in the *Autobiography* and in
Trollope's fiction: two things become identical without losing their difference, or else an identity divides without losing its oneness. This
paradoxical condition may arise within the mind, as in the case of the
castle builder who lays his own identity aside, or it may happen between
the mind and the external world, as in the case of the moral consciousness
that produces a real archdeacon without having seen one. No middle
term of communication or signification links two different things; they
are strictly two, yet also one. This magical equivalence comes into being
at a moment, a point of difference between what went before and what
follows after; yet the moment can never be precisely located because it
turns out always to have already happened. Conception of characters,
like the birth of the novelist himself, can be pinned down no more closely
than that it has already occurred before writing begins. Such situations
are paradoxical and logically impossible, but they are fundamental to
Trollope's theory of the novel, which seeks higher satisfactions than
those that logic can provide.

When the *Autobiography* deals with the making of novels, it shifts
easily from Trollope's own method to general advice on how "the

novelist" should go about his business. It is apparent, however, that the
only way to write a good novel is to do exactly what Trollope himself has
done. The success or failure of Trollope's contemporaries can also be
measured according to how closely their methods have corresponded to
his. The *Autobiography* allows considerable leeway in matters of style
and subject, but it is strict on one point, which it makes the ultimate
standard for evaluating any novel: "He [the novelist] desires to make his
readers so intimately acquainted with his characters that the creations of
his brain should be to them speaking, moving, living, human creatures.
This he can never do unless he know those fictitious personages himself,
and he can never know them well unless he can live with them in the full
reality of established intimacy" (199-200). Thackeray "lived with the
characters he was creating," and Trollope ranks him first among modern
novelists (209); Dickens, "in his best days, always lived with his characters," but when he lost the power to do so, he "ceased to charm" (214).
One has only the novels themselves to go on, but if the novels produce an
impression of life, one can be sure that the novelist's "living with" his
characters is the reason. Thackeray "must have lived in perpetual intercourse" with his best characters: "Therefore he has made these personages
real to us" (210).

   "Living with" his characters is the second stage of Trollope's own
novel making. Like the rest of his art, it is detached from the events of his
life: it begins at the indeterminate moment of conception, and it has no
determinable ending. It is not ended by the writing of the novel, nor need
it end even with the written death of the character. While writing *The
Last Chronicle of Barset*, Trollope decides to "kill" Mrs. Proudie; "but I
have never dissevered myself from Mrs. Proudie, and still live much in
company with her ghost" (238). He may lose track of a character, as he
does of Mary Lowther in *The Vicar of Bullhampton* (286), but if the
capacity for knowing characters fails, "then I shall know that the old
horse should be turned out to grass" (200). In Trollope's late letters,
written after the *Autobiography* was finished and locked away, the
insistence on total memory is repeated. A year before he died, Trollope
wrote to Arthur Tilley that he admits to having forgotten a character
only because it "looks modest; — and to do the other thing looks the
reverse." In fact, however, "the writer never forgets."[1]

   During the period of living-with, there is a gradual development of
what the *Autobiography* calls intimacy. The faculty of the novelist's

[1]Letter to Arthur Tilley, 5 December 1881, in Bradford A. Booth, ed., *The Letters of
Anthony Trollope* (London: Oxford University Press, 1951), p. 465.

mind that produces character does not "know" what it has produced; another faculty comes into operation that experiences the character as one might experience a real person whom one has met and slowly gets to know. None of this impinges on the real life of the novelist; knowing continues at a constant rate no matter what the real-life man is doing. Within his novelist self, he is divided into the knower and the thing to be known, yet this division leaves him still one. Such a multiplicity in unity produces "the full reality of established intimacy":

> They [the characters] must be with him [the novelist] as he lies down to sleep, and as he wakes from his dreams. He must learn to hate them and to love them. He must argue with them, quarrel with them, forgive them, and even submit to them. He must know of them, whether they be cold-blooded or passionate, whether true or false, and how far true, and how far false. The depth and the breadth, and the narrowness and the shallowness of each should be clear to him.

This is the only way to make a good novel, and it is how Trollope has made his own: "It is so that I have lived with my characters, and thence has come whatever success I have attained" (200).

Trollope has a fondness for dividing himself as well as his novels into stories that run parallel but do not interact. No self-division, however, is more profound than this one, which puts him perpetually in two worlds at once. The novelist's life is structured as the same sort of identity-in-difference that organizes the moment of becoming a novelist, the moment of a character's creation, and the writing of the *Autobiography*. In all these cases, unity is formed by the equivalence of two different things, when there is no mediation between them. In all these cases, too, the novelist's identity is withdrawn from the significant side of the relation and reserved in the side that should be ignored. Every day of his life the novelist pursues two equally real careers, but his identity lives in only one of them, the insignificant one. Like a novel, which contains characters to be sympathized with and plot to be overlooked, every feature of Trollope's theory involves a doubling that separates a thing of value from a thing that is said to have none yet that cannot be done away with.

In contrast to the workmanlike routine of writing, living-with has a romantically imaginative quality that, if it were not the heart of the Trollopian creative process, one would have to call un-Trollopian. Writing can be done with equal facility anywhere, but living-with is best carried on "at some quiet spot among the mountains":

> And I am sure that the work so done has had in it the best truth and the highest spirit that I have been able to produce. At such times I have been able

to imbue myself thoroughly with the characters I have had in hand. I have wandered alone among the rocks and woods, crying at their grief, laughing at their absurdities, and thoroughly enjoying their joy. I have been impregnated with my own creations till it has been my only excitement to sit with the pen in my hand, and drive my team before me at as quick a pace as I could make them travel. (151-52)

In the late essay "A Walk in a Wood" (*Good Words* 20 [1879]: 595-600), this scene of living-with is described in greater detail and made even more romantic. Now, like Homer, Cicero, and Dante, Trollope has "his Ariel," whom he must "catch" and "bind." In order for the novelist to do this, "his fancy should be undisturbed"; he requires that "the trees should overshadow him, that the birds should comfort him, that the green and yellow mosses should be in unison with him, — that the very air should be good to him" (600).

Romantic scenery like this, and poetical requirements like these, are as foreign to the rest of Trollope's practice as they are to the world of his novels. But the trees, birds, and mosses offer no inspiration, as they might if a poet rather than a novelist walked among them. By working "in unison" with the novelist, the features of nature blank themselves out, leaving him free to engage in undistracted communion with his characters. Along with nature, human society is absent from scenes like these; the whole world, in effect, has disappeared. The world must disappear so that it can be duplicated; the best way to reproduce the world is to go out from it, to a place where there is nothing to imitate.

Trollope's theory of conception involves neither recollection nor imitation. Rather, the doubled novelist (who contains both the knower and the thing to be known) brings his two halves into equivalence by letting one sympathize with the other. The process does not involve communication—the emission of signs by one faculty and their interpretation by the other—and there is no medium of any kind between the characters and the novelist. Again, there is something magical about the process: it is the peculiarly Trollopian magic of duplication without imitation, transmission without signs. As in the other cases that I have examined, the trick depends on the achievement of sameness within difference, and it gets its magical aura from being performed without the assistance of signification. Signification is the missing element in all of Trollope's paradoxes. Its absence, indeed, is what makes them paradoxical to the observer, though they are presented as if they were the most natural, the easiest things in the world.

Trollope describes his characters, and the best characters in all novels, first of all as living people. They are "men and women with flesh and blood, creatures with whom we can sympathise" (196). All his discussions of character assume a belief in its life. The creation of this belief is also a pervasive demand of mid-Victorian criticism, and Trollope distinguishes himself from his contemporaries chiefly by the intensity of his own belief and the supreme value he assigns to it in his theory. "Life," of course, is among the vaguest of terms, and no mid-Victorian critics, including Trollope, ever attempted to define it. For the most part, critics were content to point out where the belief had not been created rather than seeking to analyze the rare cases where it had. Throughout his career, for example, Wilkie Collins was chastised for having failed "to create a character which the world shall recognize as an addition to the number of living beings."[2] Mary Elizabeth Braddon, too, along with the other sensation novelists of the 1860s and 70s, was condemned for having failed to impart "living vitality" to her characters. Again in her case, though no reviewer revealed how the feeling of life was to be produced, all of them knew the feeling when they had it: "we cannot disenchant ourselves from the idea, that they who have suffered as we have suffered, sorrowed as we have sorrowed, and rejoiced as we have rejoiced, are living realities."[3]

When successful examples of living characters are cited by mid-Victorian critics, they turn out almost always to be Mrs. Poyser and Colonel Newcome, who also figure prominently in Trollope's list of characters with whom their authors have "lived." In practice, "life" was often the same as cuteness or charm. In theory, however, though its production remained obscure, the feeling of life was the chief criterion of any novel's success for Trollope and his contemporaries alike. This feeling was the heart of realism: "life" and "reality" were everywhere linked in phrases like "living reality" and "real life." Trollope uses them together and interchangeably: Thackeray "must have lived in perpetual intercourse" with his characters; therefore "he has made these personages real to us" (210). In 1859, David Masson declared that the creation of "living characters" was the ultimate achievement of any novel, and he made a timely speculation on their reality: "In a metaphysical sense, these phantoms of the human imagination are things, existences, parts of the world as it is, equally with the rocks which we tread, the trees which we see and can touch, and the clouds that sail in the blue above us. May they

[2]Review of *No Name*, *Spectator* 36 (10 January 1863): 1502.
[3]"Miss Braddon, The Illuminated Newgate Calendar," *Eclectic and Congregational Review* 14 (January 1868): 23.

not, then, have a function in the *real* evolution of the future?"[4] Few mid-Victorian critics ventured into metaphysics; for most of them, the reality of fictional characters was a simple matter of the reader's feelings. The reader must somehow be made to feel that the characters he reads about are just as alive, and therefore just as real, as he is himself. If a novel produces this feeling, it is a success; if it does not, though it may be as clever and as well written as possible, it must be second rate.

The feeling of reality is inseparable from the action of sympathy. Trollope's period of living-with his characters is a course in the cultivation of sympathy, and characters obtain "flesh and blood" by being "creatures with whom we can sympathise." Again, without indicating how sympathy is produced, mid-Victorian critics joined Trollope in demanding it from all novels; and again, they were much more acute about its absence than its presence. For Trollope, characters who do not produce sympathy are "wooden blocks" (195), and novels that lack such characters are "novels of wood" (200). For critics, characters without sympathy were often "puppets" or "lay-figures," wooden objects that, though they resemble real people, are too obviously artificial to produce the feeling of life. A desire or intention to write living characters was taken to be universal among novelists; their absence was a failure of execution, a visible gap between the novelist's design and his achievement. The gap showed itself primarily in the reader's awareness that the author was forcing his characters to do what they do, that he was their manipulator or puppeteer.

There is some ambivalence on this subject, however, in both Trollope and his contemporaries. Most often, sympathy is looked upon as an achievement of art that the novelist must strive for and that can be used as the gauge of how good a novelist he is. But sometimes sympathy is regarded as the result of an inherent power in the novel as a genre. Novels will, by their nature, elicit sympathetic responses from their readers, and the novelist's principal duty is to direct and limit sympathy, not merely to induce it.[5] Mid-Victorian critics, however, were not greatly

[4] *British Novelists and Their Styles* (Boston: Gould & Lincoln, 1859), p. 40.

[5] The latter view is, perhaps, the more traditional one. It was held, for example, by Samuel Johnson, who observed in 1750 that, in contrast to the romances of former ages,

these familiar histories may perhaps be made of greater use than the solemnities of professed morality, and convey the knowledge of vice and virtue with more efficacy than axioms and definitions. But if the power of example is so great, as to take possession of the memory by a kind of violence, and produce effects almost without the intervention of the will, care ought to be taken that, when the choice is unrestrained, the best examples only should be exhibited; and that which is likely to operate so strongly, should not be mischievous or uncertain in its effects. (*Rambler* 4)

troubled by this power in the contemporary English novel. They tended
to find it menacing mostly in foreign novels, particularly French, as their
slow acceptance of Balzac and Zola reveals. For the most part they
agreed with Trollope that the "general result" of the English novel had
always been to "make virtue alluring and vice ugly," and that this was
also the result of contemporary novels, including Trollope's (190-91).
Even the luridly wicked heroines of Miss Braddon were more often
condemned for clumsiness than for moral danger. Miss Braddon and the
other sensation novelists failed at sympathy; they might be idle, but they
were seldom called dangerous.

There were, however, some viewers-with-alarm. As Trollope remarks,
there had been until recent years an "embargo" on novels in many English
households (188); and, though the situation was steadily improving by
the 1860s, pockets of resistance remained. An interesting case of such
resistance was William Thomson, Archbishop of York, who, on 31
October 1864, delivered an address to the Huddersfield Church Institute,
condemning the sensation novel in the simplest and strongest terms. Not
only were such novels "useless," said the archbishop, but they were also
dangerous. In the perpetration of certain "great crimes," left unspecified,
he claimed to see the influence of the "kind of feeling" produced by
sensation novels.[6] Archbishop Thomson won himself a good deal of
publicity by this attack, but though he might have elicited sympathy in
the members of the Church Institute, journalists and literary critics treated
him with annoyed and embarrassed condescension. No reader is likely to
become a menace to society because he has read sensation novels,
commented the *Saturday Review*; they are "simply stories of exciting
incident, without any sort of relation to the social system." On the other
hand, however, "an archbishop is not bound to make himself pleasant."[7]

Trollope departs significantly from the ordinary critical position on
this subject. The *Autobiography* lays heavy stress on the power of novels
to influence their readers' lives, explicitly refuting the opinion that fiction
is trivial and that a taste for it is no more significant than a taste for
"pastry after dinner." Reading novels is "neither vicious nor vain"; indeed,
"a vast proportion of the teaching of the day" is done by novels, more
than by poetry and even by sermons (187-88). Teaching, for Trollope, is
the distinctive power of novels, and being taught is the distinctive effect
of reading them, whether the novelist desires it or not. He can give

[6] *The Times*, 2 November 1864, p. 9.
[7] "The Perils of Sensation," *Saturday Review* 18 (5 November 1864): 559.

pleasure in varying degrees, depending on his skill, but "he must teach whether he wish to teach or no" (190). Like plot, the power to teach is in the novel by definition, and the novelist has no choice but to accept the fact.

The presence of plot, however, is the source of special problems. Everything valuable in the novel is centered in its portrayal of character: character gives the novelist his pleasure and the reader his instruction; character elicits sympathy and recognition, which are the distinctive effects of the novel as a genre. Yet character is not the whole novel; to make a novel complete, there must also be plot. Plot is a sort of impurity in the nature of novels. It cannot be dispensed with, and the reading public has an unfortunate fondness for it, but these are facts that the world thrusts upon the novelist, and with which he must deal as best he can. Unlike character, plot gives the novelist no pleasure and the reader no benefit. One might think that the best thing to do with plot would be to eliminate it. Subsequent novelists have claimed, at least, to write "plotless" novels, and Trollope's contemporaries often accused him of having done just that. But in Trollope's theory there is no way of omitting plot. It must be there—"You must provide a vehicle of some sort" (109) —and the only way to manage this necessity is to arrange somehow that plot will be reduced to a minimum and the reader's attention will be directed as much as possible toward what ought to concern him totally —character.

For Trollope, as for his contemporaries, plot is associated with the acts of writing and reading, while character is in the represented world and the real world, conveyed across the gap between them by means of those acts. Trollope, however, goes beyond his contemporaries (who just as frequently criticized him for providing too little plot as they criticized Wilkie Collins for providing too much) in wishing to efface the gap between the represented and the real so completely that the intervening elements will seem to disappear. I have shown that, in Trollope's theory, both the characters and the novelist's knowledge of them are complete before any writing is done. Trollope also judges the success of all novels according to how well they re-create this completeness in the mind of the reader. It would be well, perhaps, if this equivalence could be achieved magically, as similar equivalences are achieved in the conception of character. Unfortunately, however, writing and reading must intervene. They form an inescapable middle term that, like plot, is necessary but irksome. These mediations do not trouble the author's conception of his characters or his living-with them, but in order that the characters might be duplicated in the reader's experience, they must be translated into language, then out of it again.

Trollope and his contemporaries agree that concentration on plot requires neglect of character. Statements like this were common in reviews of the 1860s and 70s: "The worst effect of sensational 'proclivities' is, as a rule, their effect on a novelist's characters,"[8] and this criticism of *No Name* makes a typical connection: *"No Name* has all the faults, but it has all the merits, of this kind of fiction. It is a mere puzzle, in which the artist moves his puppets so as to make us wonder what is to be the end of them. We do not care, and are not meant to care, about the characters of the story."[9] No periodical reviewer went to the trouble of establishing a theory to account for this imbalance within the novel, but most of them recognized its effects. Generally, critics were content to describe the novel as a sort of vessel, into which a limited amount of compositional liquid could be poured. Plot and character, like oil and water, could be combined but never fused. Any increase in one component necessitated a decrease in the other. Often, the novelist was said to contain the imbalance: he had a limited amount of energy to pump into a novel, and what ran to plot had to be withheld from character. Wherever the source was located, there were two ingredients in all novels, and the one was alien and even hostile to the other.

This hostility is reflected in the incommensurate metaphors used by both Trollope and his contemporaries to describe plot and character. Plot is most often a "chain" or a "thread"; it is linear and sequential, and it has a certain power of movement as link is added to link or as the thread is followed from beginning to end. Character is usually a "sketch" or a "painting"; it is two-dimensional, covering a surface, and though the addition of one stroke after another implies a certain successiveness, the result is the formation of a total portrait, not the movement from one point to another. There is an inherent difficulty in reconciling the two figures or in devising a composite figure that would incorporate both. The problem can be partially solved, however, by calling plot a conveyance that moves along its path carrying a burden of character. This is the solution of Stendhal's famous figure of the novel as a mirror being carried along a highway (*Red and Black*, bk. 1, 13), and in *Thackeray* (1879), Trollope devises a figure that is reminiscent, in its homelier way, of Stendhal's: "The arrangement of the words is as though you were

<hr>

[8] Review of *The Clyffards of Clyffe, Saturday Review* 20 (9 December 1865): 742.
[9] Review of *No Name, Saturday Review* 15 (17 January 1863): 84.

walking simply along a road. The arrangement of your story is as though you were carrying a sack of flour while you walked."[10] Such compound metaphors must be makeshift, and it takes very little interrogation to prove any of them inadequate. Most mid-Victorian reviewers, however, let the implications of their metaphors be what they would, so long as the primary point was made: plot and character are different, external to each other, and of unequal value.

Character, as a sketch or a painting, is mimetic, while plot, as a chain or a thread, is not. The order in which a painter applies brush strokes is invisible in the finished portrait and of no importance to it. What is important is that the finished portrait, as a whole, duplicates a structure in the world that was complete before the painting began. That structure, a human face, does not come into being during the painting of it, and the painting is good only insofar as it corresponds to the reality that is its original. Plot, in contrast, is nothing but sequence and order. Metaphors of plot come closer to describing the process of reading or writing a novel—moving from sentence to sentence and page to page. Metaphors of character describe better the recreation of reality that is supposed to be the aim of those processes—reassembling a preexisting whole that is already there and that the novel will have done justice to only when all its brush strokes have been applied. Plot is, therefore, neither constitutive of character nor necessary to it. The value of a novel depends on the degree of correspondence between its representation and the represented whole. In theory, at least, any number of possible plots could be used to convey precisely the same character.

The spatiality of character, as opposed to the linearity of plot, is an important feature of Trollope's theory. Characters are, of course, supposed to be real people, and Trollope often speaks of them as if they were. But he just as often figures them as areas of a surface, determined in their verisimilitude by the skill with which the novelist has drawn their limits. In the *Autobiography*, character is frequently a portrait: the chief merit of *The Warden*, for example, is that in it "I had realised to myself a series of portraits, and had been able so to put them on the canvas that my readers should see that which I meant them to see" (85). In any novel, if it is worth looking at, "the canvas should be crowded with real portraits" (109). The reality of such portraits, however, depends less on any positive quality in them than on their maintenance within realistic limits. Readers will recognize "human beings like to themselves" only if the characters

[10] *Thackeray* (New York: Harper & Brothers, 1879), p. 120.

show "not more of excellence" than the average amount that any reader might be supposed to own. If the characters are too fine, or if they demonstrate "exaggerated baseness," readers will lose sympathy. Instead, they will "feel themselves to be carried away among gods or demons" (125).

The major risk confronting the painter of character is not the threat of deficiency but the threat of excess. The greatest danger is that he will fall, as Trollope's mother did, into "the pitfalls of exaggeration" (28). Some sort of restraint is necessary; restraint is more important, in Trollope's account of all phases òf novel making, than the creative energy that originates and sustains the process. There is no danger to Trollope in the hypothetical case of the novelist who has written himself out (197-99); shortages never threaten the Trollopian novelist. Much more to the point is the possibly apocryphal example of the writer who "spawned" three novels a year, overburdening his publisher and his readers with "the fecundity of the herring" (95). Trollope first hears of this prodigy in 1857, and he is mentioned three more times in the *Autobiography*. Like the allure of plot, the charm of exaggeration must be resisted everywhere. Whatever it is in character that might be oversupplied, excess is the greatest danger of all, because it spoils the moral effect that only sympathy with character produces and on which the whole value of novels depends. Excess in character would lead the reader into forbidden regions: "The regions of absolute vice are foul and odious. . . . In these he [the novelist] will hardly tread. But there are outskirts on these regions, on which sweet-smelling flowers seem to grow, and grass to be green. It is in these border-lands that the danger lies" (190). Again in the matter of character, Trollope's theory describes the novel as a balancing of opposing forces, one of which pulls outward into danger while the other pulls inward toward success and safety.

I will return to the question of excess and transgression of boundaries in the next chapter, when I discuss Trollope's theory of writing. Long before writing begins, however, while the novelist is still living-with his characters, lines must be drawn to contain them. Getting to know his own creations is a process of de-fining them, setting limits that mark their outlines. It is in keeping with the figure of character as a drawing that it should be sketched in on a surface. This does not accord, however, with the figure of character as living reality, which Trollope's theory also maintains. The "full reality of established intimacy," which ought to precede all writing, has this trace of writing in it. Trollope's use of the term "character," the most important part of novel making, which precedes and follows writing but is never in it, contains this reminder of its older meaning—a letter, a written sign. In a sense, even when he has not yet picked up his pen, Trollope is already writing.

Writing

TROLLOPE'S THEORY LOCATES all the novelist's art and all his joy in a time before any writing is done. The value of a novel belongs after writing, in its effect on the reader, and that effect depends on the degree to which the latter experience duplicates the former. In the relations between novelist, characters, and reader, writing appears as a gap or interruption between the latter two. Novelist and characters encounter each other directly, within the multiple unity of the novelist's mind, where the knower and the known can come into equivalence without signification. The reader, however, cannot exactly duplicate this intimacy. In order to approach the novelist's relation to his characters, the reader must get back to the time before signification, so that he can live-with the characters as the novelist did and does. It is the greatest impurity in the novel-machine that the reader must pass through the text. He must be persuaded to overcome, or to ignore, the irreducible difference between the novel as conceived and the novel as read. That difference is writing.

Trollope's incredible system of writing is the most famous feature of the *Autobiography*. If there is such a thing as a "normal" way to write novels, it can only be the norm of exceptionality, the ground that all novelists share because most people do not write novels. But Trollope's way of writing may be the most abnormal of all, an exception to the exception. The *Autobiography* never claims that Trollope has done his writing just as any other novelist would. Rather, it says that he writes in the manner of one who is anything but a novelist. Artists are allowed to be eccentric, to suffer sudden illuminations and to wander weeping and laughing through the woods. Before he begins to write, Trollope is very artistic. While writing, however, he is less artistic than any shoemaker. Any shoemaker might safely grant himself the luxury of pausing to remark, when a pair of shoes is finished, "There is my pair of shoes finished at last! What a pair of shoes it is!" But the shoemaker-novelist dares not make such a pause. If he did, he would be "without wages half his time" (277). The Trollopian writer is much less artistic than any artist and much more severe on himself than any craftsman. He makes himself operate with the predictable regularity of a machine.

Throughout the *Autobiography*, there is a rhetorical campaign against the specialness of the novelist, whether he is Anthony Trollope or the novel writer in general. Trollope himself is "insignificant," and though he does refer to the making of novels as "my art," he never refers to himself as an artist. Early in his career, after three failed novels and an unproduced play, he still is "never troubled" by the idea that he is "the unfortunate owner of unappreciated genius" (73). Even later, when a series of successes has led some people to suppose that he might be "a man of genius," he emphatically (though deviously) denies it:

> I have never fancied myself to be a man of genius, but had I been so I think I might well have subjected myself to these trammels. Nothing surely is so potent as a law that may not be disobeyed. It has the force of the water-drop that hollows the stone. A small daily task, if it be really daily, will beat the labours of a spasmodic Hercules. It is the tortoise which always catches the hare. The hare has no chance. He loses more time in glorifying himself for a quick spurt than suffices for the tortoise to make half his journey. (103-4)

Surely no man of genius would ever unleash such a barrage of clichés, nor would he tiresomely explain the meaning of images that every child is familiar with. Trollope does this; therefore he is no genius. But if he were a man of genius, he would have acted just as he has done, subjecting himself to the trammels that disqualify him from the title. And the trammels are self-imposed. There is no deficiency in Trollope, but rather the threat of excess; and there is nothing to limit the excess but restraints that Trollope himself has devised. Only a man of genius would have to work so hard to keep from looking like one.

To some degree, Trollope's apparent belittling of the novelist is directed against the cult of personality that was an important feature of mid-Victorian literary criticism, as it had been of Romantic poetic theory.

The novelist had not yet turned into such a remarkable creature as the poet, but he was in the process of doing so; the first popular successes of such "artistic" novelists as Meredith, Hardy, and James occurred about the time the *Autobiography* was written, though it mentions none of them. Trollope insists on a sharp distinction between the poet and the novelist, and his stance can be read as a defiance of the contemporary trend toward merging them under the title "genius." The difference between the two, for Trollope, is that the novelist resists the temptations to which the poet gives himself over. Among these attractive errors is the tendency to treat "poet" and "poetry" as if they were synonyms, a mistake that derives from the assumption that poems are signs of genius, that the excellence of poetry is a symptom of the excellence of the poet.[1] If the poet accepts this connection, he may seek to achieve the former excellence by cultivating the latter—treating himself as an extraordinary being, broadcasting himself to the world through his poems. The Trollopian novelist must never do this: even his autobiography contains as little as possible of himself, and he becomes a novelist when he lays his identity aside. Despite what may seem his oppressive personal presence in his novels, Trollope in theory requires personal absence. In its own perverse way, the theory resembles the cult of impersonality that James developed in his prefaces and that was favored by other post-Trollopian novelists like Zola and Joyce.[2]

The major difference between the poet and the novelist, for Trollope, lies in their methods of writing—not in what they do beforehand, or even in the effect their writing produces. The Trollopian scene of living-with contains as much poetical self-communion as any more artistic artist could claim. Its glamor is heightened by the exclusion of inspiration, so

[1] In *English Poetic Theory, 1825-1865* (Princeton: Princeton University Press, 1950), A. H. Warren observes that early Victorian critics "tended to regard the particular poem rather as a sign and instrument, a simple medium of qualities in the poet or effects in the reader, than anything of final value in and for itself" (p. 215). The result is that "the morality of art is placed squarely, in theory at least, in the character of the poet—which, by the way, is probably where it belongs" (p. 222). Trollope, too, places the value of a text both before and after the text itself. But the "before" is the scene of living-with, not the writer. On this point he disagrees with his contemporaries, and with A. H. Warren.

[2] Trollope is not a genius, but many of the traits that he claims for the novelist have been ascribed by other writers precisely to men of genius. Unself-consciousness, if not impersonality, is one of these. It is important in Ruskin's account of the artistic process and in Coleridge's description of men of genius in all ages. In Coleridge's words, it is "an essential mark of true genius that its sensibility is excited by any other cause more powerfully than by its own personal interests; for this plain reason, that the man of genius lives most in the ideal world . . . and because his feelings have been habitually associated with thoughts and images, to the number, clearness, and vivacity of which the sensation of self is always in an inverse proportion" (*Biographia Literaria*, 2).

that the equivalence of the imagined and the real comes about by magic rather than by communication or copying. Poetry and novels also have the same "end"—to teach—and their teaching is "of the same nature" (186). In the latter area, the two genres differ only in their success: novels do exactly what poetry does, but they do it better. It is a persistent theme in Trollope's critical writings that novels have "replaced" poetry as the most effective and popular literary genre. Bluntly stated, poetry is just too difficult to bother with, when the same benefits can be had more easily from novels: "I do not say that lessons such as these may not be more grandly taught by higher flights than mine. Such lessons come to us from our greatest poets. But there are so many who will read novels and understand them, who either do not read the works of our great poets, or reading them miss the lesson!" (126). Poetry is outmoded, and its way of being written is responsible.

There is certainly no shortage of praise in Trollope's discussions of poetry. The *Autobiography* always speaks of poetry in terms of awe, as if Trollope sincerely wished to take "higher flights" but has been held back by a shortage of genius that he modestly admits to. But Trollope's rhetoric is least to be trusted when it aims at (and creates) a self-deprecating impression. There is nothing modest about Trollope's claims for the power of the novel, nor is there any self-deprecation in naming his own method as that by which all novels should be constructed. Trollope is an accomplished rhetorician, whose forte is saying opposite things at the same time, and his rhetoric is at its subtlest when it claims that something has been done because a certain power or supply was lacking. The primary mechanism of the Trollopian novel-machine is the enforcement of limitations on energies that threaten to exceed the limits set on them. The excess is never more troublesome than when it is called a shortage.

Such is prominently the case in the opposition between the poet and the novelist, as the following virtuoso passage illustrates:

> By the common consent of all mankind who have read, poetry takes the highest place in literature. That nobility of expression, and all but divine grace of words, which she is bound to attain before she can make her footing good, is not compatible with prose. Indeed it is that which turns prose into poetry. When that has been in truth achieved, the reader knows that the writer has soared above the earth, and can teach his lessons somewhat as a god might teach. He who sits down to write his tale in prose makes no such attempt, nor does he dream that the poet's honour is within his reach;—but his teaching is of the same nature, and his lessons all tend to the same end. (186)

The praise is hardly faint, but it is damning. The weakly personified, feminine poetry cuts a ludicrous figure, soaring above the earth while trying to make her footing good. The masculine novelist, working toward the same goal, sits down to write. Trollope always describes poetry in terms of flying, but he also always figures life, reality, character—the things that matter—as belonging to the earth. Poetry may soar in order to become godlike, but if sympathy is her aim it is a mistake to think that she can achieve it by making herself different from anything human.

Poetry is an addition to prose, a supplement to it. Poetry may be more ancient than prose, and therefore more venerable, but she is not more original. She comes into being when prose has been inflated (or inspired) by a blast of what can be nothing but hot air. The inflation happens, furthermore, during the writing, not the conception, of what is to be conveyed. Poets and novelists are the same in the scene of living-with; their difference comes about in the scene of writing. Writing is a supplement to a community free of signification, but the novelist tries hard to make the supplement disappear between the equivalent experiences of writer and reader. The poet distinguishes himself from the novelist by heightening this difference instead of effacing it. He takes off from the common ground that novelists and readers share, enforcing instead of attempting to reduce the unavoidable difference between writers and readers. Because he desires to teach like a god rather than like a man, he adds his self-personality to a relation that would be complete without it—a relation that becomes complete, for the novelist, when he lays his self-personality aside. Poetry is the written assertion of writing, the very thing that constitutes the novelist by its effacement.

Trollope's apparent praise of poetry has the surreptitious effect of exiling it from the scene of human life. That life, for Trollope, is enacted on the real ground where characters and people walk. The old image of the poet as a bird, or some sort of flying creature, acquires in Trollope's use a pejorative emphasis. Tennyson's eagle has a commanding view of the "azure world" from its mountain crag, and the sun-treading Shelley is in every way superior to the earth-bound Browning who cherishes signs of his flight; but to soar above the earth is also to interpose a space between oneself and one's fellow beings, and it is this aspect of the figure that Trollope's rhetoric emphasizes. The poet lifts himself and his writing "somewhat into the clouds" (126); though the feat inspires awe, it cripples sympathy. Everything in the novelist's enterprise aims at establishing equivalence and reducing distances. The poet, who wants to achieve the same goal, pursues it by the perverse and willful means of flying away from his readers. If the poet must soar, Trollope is willing to let him rule over misty vistas, so long as he leaves to the novelist the real, solid earth on which people live.[3]

The difference between the poet and the novelist, for Trollope, is confined to the way they write, but it is not specifically that one writes verse and the other prose. Rather, it is that the poet directs much more attention than the novelist to the language he uses. Poetry is known by its "all but divine grace of words," not by anything celestial in its meaning. This grace is an impediment to character: George Eliot (whose poetry Trollope "will not attempt to speak of") no longer produces characters like Mrs. Poyser, because now "the author soars to things which seem to her to be higher than Mrs. Poyser." Soaring is free flight, but its effect is constriction. George Eliot now "lacks ease," and her struggles with her own language beget in the reader "a flavour of affectation" (212). It is a curious feature of Trollope's treatment of this subject that, though his own and other properly written novels stimulate in the reader only a general "sense" or "feeling" of reality, anything written poetically is said to taste or smell bad. "A man who thinks much of his words as he writes will generally leave behind him work that smells of oil." If we like this smell, then we like poetry: "in poetry we know what care is necessary, and we form our tastes accordingly" (152-53). The poet's work stinks of labor, but also of the laborer, who asserts his identity as he writes instead of laying it aside as the Trollopian writer has done. A similar problem affects the works of Wilkie Collins; in reading them, Trollope "can never lose the taste of the construction." The construction is "minute and most wonderful," but "such work gives me no pleasure" (220-21).

[3]In this case, too, Trollope's theory conforms to a cliché of mid-Victorian criticism. Critics also banished the poet from the scene of life. As Alexander Smith wrote in 1863:

> The provinces of prose and verse may be very strictly defined. Verse can deal with the tent of Achilles, prose with the modern drawing-room or dinner-table. . . . The range of verse is narrower if higher than the range of prose. Verse deals with the mountain peaks of passion, so to speak, —prose with the lower slopes and the level plain, on which stand towns and cities, and to which the experience of the majority of mankind is confined. Men are moved deepest by that which touches them most closely; and the novel, in so far as it concerns itself with modern social relationships with which readers are inevitably brought in contact . . . is naturally more popular than the poem which, by an innate necessity, must deal with the simpler and intenser emotions, and with these stripped of prosaic modern circumstances with which all are familiar. ("Novels and Novelists of the Day," North British Review 38 [February 1863]: 170-71)

The exile of the poet is called for even more floridly by David Masson in British Novelists and Their Styles (Boston: Gould & Lincoln, 1859), pp. 30-31. A practicing poet's angry response to attitudes like these can be seen in Matthew Arnold's preface of 1853, and in book 1 of The Ring and the Book, which declares itself to be the reappropriation of "a novel country; I might make it mine" (1348).

Successful realism and minute attention to details of language are not incompatible, as Flaubert's example shows. But in Trollope's theory they are so different that they exclude one another. This difference allows the odd pairing of poetry and the sensation novel—two kinds of writing that in all other respects are unlike each other, but that share an improper obsession with language. Both of them are opposed to realistic writing. This unlikely conjunction resembles another—that of what Trollope calls "plot," with its associations of linearity and movement, and what he calls "poetry," with its assertion of self and its unpleasant aura of oil. All these things are centered on writing, and all of them are subject to exclusion and restraint. In this sense, poetry and plot are representatives of writing, that stage in the novel-making process that cannot be eliminated, but that ought to be reduced as far as possible. This is not to say that Trollope's theory advocates the neglect of writing, but writing is always to be scheduled, arranged, and regulated—never indulged in. The major difference between the realist and all other dealers in language is that the realist has thoroughly tamed his medium, while the others have all, in some degree, surrendered to it.

In the *Autobiography*, writing belongs to the narrative of Trollope's life, the "insignificant" part of the book. Anthony Trollope has written his novels in a certain way, which he describes at length; but the writing, like all other real-life activities, is unimportant compared to Trollope's theoretical mechanism of character and sympathy. Writing, however, ought to be the link between life and art. It is the means by which the parallel world of Trollope's characters is translated into a commodity that circulates in the real world and makes the real world possible. The relation is circular and economic: characters are translated into writing, writing becomes books that are translated into money, and money sustains the novelist's life, permitting him to continue producing characters. Nothing is lost in any of these translations, and only the death of the novelist ought to be able to shut the machine down. Again, however, there are temptations. The novel-writing profession is the most "charming" career a man can assume, because the novelist is "subject to no bonds such as those which bind other men." He is "free from all shackle as to hours"; he can write whenever and wherever he pleases (180). But this charming freedom is also dangerous. It may lead to the erroneous belief that authors "are relieved from the necessity of paying attention to everyday rules" (282). Since there is no external force to bind the writer down, Trollope has subjected himself to "certain self-imposed laws" that he recommends to all those who wish to become novelists (102).

Trollope never specifies what his laws are intended to control, but they are so numerous and so strict that they seem to cancel whatever special freedom the novelist might have, hemming him in more narrowly than a galley slave. The novelist's labor "should never be allowed to become spasmodic" (102). In spite of common opinion, he should never "allow himself to wait till—inspiration moves him. When I have heard such doctrine preached, I have hardly been able to suppress my scorn" (104). The most important point is that the novelist must "give himself the habit of regarding his work as a normal condition of his life"; he must "bring himself to look at his work as does any other workman." The writer is like a shoemaker or a tallow chandler, with nothing divine or birdlike about him, getting more benefit from a piece of cobbler's wax on his chair than from the spasmodic inspiration that comes to poets (105). These lowly comparisons apply to the novelist only when he sits down to write. Trollope's estimation of the novel-making profession as a whole is extremely high, even grandiose, and the *Autobiography* is emphatic about "the dignity of the position which he [the novelist] ought to wish to assume" (230). But, like the novels he produces, the novelist is necessarily flawed. In novels, the flaw is plot; in novel production, it is writing. Both require being kept within bounds—not because they are useless or barren, but because they are tempting.

Again in its discussion of writing, the *Autobiography* combines its narrative of what Anthony Trollope has done with its recommendations of what all novelists ought to do. There is also no indication that this method of writing was imitated from anyone, or even that it developed during Trollope's career. Trollopian writing is consistent, uniform, and unchanging. It begins every morning at 5:30 and goes on for three hours. The first half hour is devoted to rereading the previous day's work; the remaining time is taken up by the production of 250 words every fifteen minutes. This production is supervised by a watch: "I have found that 250 words have been forthcoming as regularly as my watch went" (234-35). In preparation for this, however, writing has been preregulated even more strictly:

> When I have commenced a new book, I have always prepared a diary, divided into weeks, and carried on for the period which I have allowed myself for the completion of the work. In this I have entered, day by day, the number of pages I have written, so that if at any time I have slipped into idleness for a day or two, the record of that idleness has been there, staring me in the face, and demanding of me increased labour, so that the deficiency might be supplied. (102-3)

Forty pages per week is the average demand, though production has ranged between 20 and 112. Furthermore, because *page* is "an ambiguous term," it has been defined to mean 250 words (103). At times of particular intensity—those times among the birds and mosses when living-with is also specially intense—the ordinary output of 8 pages a day has been doubled and the work week has been extended from five days to seven (151). Even in times of stress and distraction—on trains (89), on shipboard (102), in Egypt (105)—writing goes on at a regular pace.

The *Autobiography* makes writing seem an unpleasant task, to which the novelist must be compelled by cobbler's wax and guilt. Here again, however, as in the other cases where a deficiency is claimed, the implicit threat is excess. Regulation is imposed not to coax an unwilling writer to work but to prevent him from writing too much:

> This division of time allowed me to produce over ten pages of an ordinary novel volume a day, and if kept up through ten months, would have given as its result three novels of three volumes each in the year;—the precise amount which so greatly acerbated the publisher in Paternoster Row, and which must at any rate be felt to be quite as much as the novel-readers of the world can want from the hands of one man. (235)

Even with all his restraints, Trollope was frequently criticized in the 1860s and 70s for glutting the novel market. The failure of *He Knew He Was Right* in 1869, which I shall discuss in detail in chapter 8, seemed to prove that he had done so. In both life and theory, the unnamed over-producer who disgusted everybody with his fecundity is a far more disturbing prospect than the worn-out hack who must glue himself to his chair lest he not write enough. The problem of overproduction is ultimately solved only by a detour: novels may be written at a rate far in excess of the world's demand, but they can be stored away in Trollope's desk and published at safe intervals. At the time the *Autobiography* was written, three novels were finished and waiting (235); at the time of Trollope's death, the *Autobiography* and two more novels were left behind.

In addition to these self-devised restraints, Trollopian writing borrows limitations from the world of novel publishing. What for a more artistic novelist might be irksome mechanical requirements become for Trollope a trustworthy schedule of supply and demand. But in several cases the schedule was more the novelist's invention than his publisher's. Referring to *The Last Chronicle of Barset* (on which he had been working for about two weeks), Trollope made this accommodating, if bewildering, offer to George Smith:

I commonly divide a number of 32 pages (such as the numbers of 'Orley Farm') into four chapters each. If you wish the work to be so arranged as to run either to 20 or to 30 numbers, I must work each of the 20 numbers by 6 chapters, taking care that the chapters run so equally, two and two, as to make each four into one equal part or each six into one equal part—There will be some trouble in this, but having a mechanical mind I think I can do it.[4]

Whatever Smith may have made of this proposal, *The Last Chronicle* was published in thirty-two weekly numbers, containing two, three, or four chapters. Trollope always claims, in the *Autobiography* and elsewhere, that the convenience of publishers and readers is the sole motive for the complex calibration of his output. The calibration, however, precedes any specific external demand for it; and sometimes, as in this case, it bears little relation to the plan of the novel's actual publication.

Writing seems to offer no resistance to Trollope's multiple scales of measurement; it is submissive to division in any number of ways. Only a very uniform substance can be divided according to so many alternative plans. Trollope describes writing as if it were the constant, regular emission of a fluid: the fluid will fill a vessel of any size or shape without a change in its own nature. Writing has no structure of its own; it never dictates how it will be measured. And, because it has no inner structure —no self-personality, perhaps—it can mold itself to any other structure that might be imposed upon it, either by what it conveys (the fictional world of characters) or by how it is manifested (in the real world of publishers and readers). Writing has nothing to say for itself; like a machine, it can turn itself neither on nor off. It has, however, the paradoxical power of submissiveness. It is ready to be divided up in any way at all, but it compels division, because without the imposition of limit and measure it would flow formlessly forever.

In contrast to the sensation novelist and the poet, the realist pays no attention to writing while he is doing it. A great deal of care is necessary beforehand, but writing itself should be as close as possible to automatic:

There is a good deal to be learned by any one who wishes to write a novel well; but when the art has been acquired, I do not see why two or three should not be well written at the same time. I have never found myself thinking much about the work that I had to do till I was doing it. I have indeed for many years almost abandoned the effort to think, trusting myself, with the narrowest thread of plot, to work the matter out when the pen is in my hand. (134)

---

[4]Letter to George Smith, 6 February 1866, in Bradford A. Booth, ed., *The Letters of Anthony Trollope* (London: Oxford University Press, 1951), p. 178.

All of Trollope's restrictions on words apply to their number, none to their nature. Though the size of the work to be done is planned carefully in advance and watched over carefully in progress, the choice of what the words will be needs no preparation or supervision. The faster the writing can be done, the better the result will be: "the work which has been done the quickest has been done the best" (150). But quickness is a virtue only in writing; the best novels come from "hot pressure, not in the conception, but in the telling of the story" (151).

Within its limits of time and quantity, writing is allowed to run free. The more quickly the writing is done, the more authentic it is—a principle that is valid for all kinds of writing, not just for novels. Trollope writes his travel books this way, as, for example, *The West Indies and the Spanish Main:* "The fact memorable to me now is that I never made a single note while writing or preparing it. Preparation, indeed, there was none. The descriptions and opinions came hot on to the paper from their causes" (112). Even Trollope's Post Office reports are written "without a copy":

> It is by writing thus that a man can throw on to his paper the exact feeling with which his mind is impressed at the moment. A rough copy, or what is called a draft, is written in order that it may be touched and altered and put upon stilts. The waste of time, moreover, in such an operation, is terrible. If a man knows his craft with his pen, he will have learned to write without the necessity of changing his words or the form of his sentences. I had learned so to write my reports that they who read them should know what it was that I meant them to understand. (116-17)

To write quickly is to write well: "it is the best way of producing to the eye of the reader, and to his ear, that which the eye of the writer has seen and his ear heard" (112).

It might seem odd that speed and lack of forethought should produce accuracy of expression. They would seem, by ordinary standards, to impede accuracy rather than to assure it, and the care with which a novelist revises and reforms his language has traditionally been taken as a standard of praise rather than blame. Trollope, of course, does not counsel negligence. Indeed, his demands upon the novelist as a writer are numerous and very severe. But all of them are to be met without the assistance of any writing that falls short of complete accuracy. The novelist pays great attention to his language, but he does so either before he picks up his pen or while he is writing exactly the words that the world will see. Unlike the sensation novelist, the poet, or the misguided writer of Post Office reports, the realist produces no half-written work that would have to be supplemented or rewritten. Writing never assists writing; all the words come "hot on to the paper from their causes."

Words so written are correct. For that reason, they should never need to be changed. Trollope reads over all his work four times, three times in manuscript and once in print, checking for grammatical errors (153). Correcting them, however, alters nothing in the nature of what is conveyed. Grammar is an act of courtesy, not an aspect of meaning. Readers expect the novelist to obey certain rules, "and unless he does obey them, he will disgust" (152). But the words themselves are permanent and permanently true. Until writing becomes public, it also remains almost absolutely private. There should be "no intercourse at all" between novelists and critics, except the encounter of novel and critical review (229), and only Trollope's wife is allowed to read any of his writing before it is printed (63). The writer and his writing are as different as they can be, but at the same time what the writer writes is uniquely his own. With the exception of *Doctor Thorne*, whose plot was supplied by Trollope's brother (99), "I have never consulted a friend as to a plot, or spoken to any one of the work I have been doing" (63). With the added exception of the legal opinion on heirlooms in *The Eustace Diamonds*, "I have never printed as my own a word that has been written by others" (100).

The permanent accuracy of the written word contrasts strongly with the living fluidity of the stages that precede and follow writing. Living-with his characters puts the novelist in dynamic relation to them, a relation that never turns static but continues to deepen and change even after the novel has been written. The reader's encounter with the characters should have the same quality of living development. He should feel that, as time passes in the novel, the characters gradually age (200), and there should always be a sense of freedom, or of jeopardy, about what course the characters will take. Nothing is worse, in reading, than that the "course of the tale" should seem to be "one piece of stiff mechanism, in which there is no room for a doubt" (199). For the writer, it is only at the moment of writing that fixation occurs. Until then, the novelist himself is as ignorant as his future readers of what the characters will do next — of what, in effect, the next words will be.

In the *Autobiography*, Trollope denies prearrangement of the two events in his fiction that seem most to bear its mark, the death of Mrs. Proudie (237-38) and the theft of the Eustace diamonds (296). In "A Walk in a Wood," he adds to these denials that of another suspicious case, Lady Mason's confession in *Orley Farm*: "I wrote a novel once in which a lady forged a will; but I had not myself decided that she had forged it till the chapter before that in which she confesses her guilt" (595). Wilkie Collins is called upon to make contrast: "All these things, and many more, Wilkie Collins could have arranged before with infinite labour, preparing things present so that they should fit in with things to come. I have gone on the very much easier plan of making everything as it comes fit in with what has gone before" (296). The realistic novelist thinks a great deal about his novel before he begins to write, but he never determines the words until they are permanently set down. The sensationalist, his opposite, has prearrenged everything, prewritten it.

The difference has nothing to do with ease. It is enforced by the same principle that sets the Trollopian novelist apart from such diverse opposites as the poet and the Post Office employee who makes a first draft. These writers have in common with the sensation novelist that they put on paper words that are not exact—whether the form be a plot outline, an early version of a poem, or a first draft of a report. All of them are willing, then, to transform this writing by means of other writing—filling in the outline, refining meter and metaphor, polishing phrases. Such nonrealistic writers treat words as words; they deal with words in their interrelations, apart from their connections to the things they signify. For the Trollopian realist, writing is valuable only because it is necessary to make the reader's experience of the characters as similar as possible to the novelist's experience of them before he begins to write. But there is no value in intertextuality. Indeed, there is less than no value in it, because the admission of an intertextual relation does harm to the achievement of equivalence that is the goal of the whole novel business. If any participant in that business considers a text as a text, then reality has been compromised. All the opponents of Trollopian realism, various as they are among themselves, share the antirealistic habit of admitting that writing has value as writing, rather than as the pure conveyance of what is other than itself.

In claiming that novels should be written spontaneously, Trollope aligns himself with Scott and Thackeray and opposes himself to Dickens and Wilkie Collins. Dickens made elaborate if idiosyncratic plans for many of his novels, and Collins bragged repeatedly about the care with which even the smallest details of his fiction had been worked out in advance. *The Woman in White* was even written "backwards," the greater part of volume 3 being composed first and volumes 1 and 2 then coordinated with it.[5] Thackeray's plots, according to Trollope, never did

---

[5]Edmund Yates, *Celebrities at Home: Third Series* (London: Office of "The World," 1879), p. 153.

"occupy so much of his mind" (209); and in the introductory epistle to
The Fortunes of Nigel, the Author of Waverly admits that he "cannot
form a plot."[6] The bias in favor of spontaneous writing is also prominent
in many mid-Victorian critics. Critics often complained that the typical
sensation novel was, in Trollope's phrase, "one piece of stiff mechanism,"
and they usually found that overpreparation was the reason for this
failure.

Because the careful prearrangement of the sensation novel was aimed
at setting traps for the reader, critics also found a degree of dishonesty in
the care. "All these stories are open to the same criticism," wrote Sir
J. F. Stephen in 1864: "Those that hide can find. The person who invented
the riddle and knows the explanation is of course able to pretend to
discover it by almost any steps, or by what really amounts to no steps at
all, and thus he can easily convey the impression of the exercise of any
amount of sagacity."[7] Implied in such criticisms is the notion that the
reader's experience of the fiction, which is focused primarily on character, should duplicate the novelist's experience—a duplication that is also
Trollope's aim. Any careful preplanning, particularly the minute attention
to plot that was distinctive of Collins and the other sensationalists, spoils
the duplication and makes the relation of writer to reader insincere. It
also unduly magnifies the writer—a fault that Trollope finds in poetry as
well as sensation novels—because the reader is challenged to duplicate
the elegance of a finished product, without benefit of the prewritten
outlines that made that elegance possible.

No critic, however, went so far as to say that novels should be made
up as they go along. Trollope not only says this, but he claims that they
must be so written if they are to be worth reading. According to Trollope,
if the novelist confines all his care to the time of living-with—a time that
is innocent of signification—and if he writes automatically, driven by the
"hot pressure" of that living and focusing all his attention on it, then the
reader will be as undistracted by the medium as the novelist has been.
All direct attention to writing opens a gap in the writer's awareness. Self-
personality asserts itself just where it ought to be laid aside; the writer
turns to his writing and away from what that writing is supposed to
convey. The gap leaves an unmistakable trace in his writing, and the

[6]Scott confided to his journal in 1825 the Trollopian confession that "I have generally
written to the middle of one of these novels, without having the least idea how it was to
[end]" (quoted in Edgar Johnson, *Sir Walter Scott: The Great Unknown* [New York:
Macmillan Co., 1970], p. 1044). Trollope's statements on novel writing as a profession often
recall Scott's. The advantages of rapid work and the respectability of writing for money are
emphasized by both.

[7]"Detectives in Fiction and in Real Life," *Saturday Review* 17 (11 June 1864): 713.

reader perceives it as that "smell of oil" that characterizes poetry. The reader never notices realistic writing, because the writer never noticed it. When a novelist writes automatically, "the language is always lucid. The reader, without labour, knows what he means, and knows all that he means" (210). The novelist's identity, his language, and his plot, all disappear from everybody's awareness. What remains is clear, immediate perception of character—just as clear for the reader as it was for the novelist before he started writing.

The *Autobiography* gives a good deal of advice to the aspiring novelist on the handling of language, which "must of course be to him a matter of much consideration." But that consideration is all taken care of before any writing is done, and its aim is to make language invisible: "It is not sufficient that there be a meaning which may be hammered out of the sentence, but that the language should be so pellucid that the meaning should be rendered without an effort to the reader;—and not only some proportion of meaning, but the very sense, no more and no less, which the writer has intended to put into his words" (201). Transparency and accuracy are the same; when language completely conveys its meaning, it disappears and only meaning remains. That meaning is character and sympathy—equivalence established without the intervention of signs.

Language is not lucid by nature; the novelist must work to make it so by becoming "a severe critic to himself" (202). Poets, sensation novelists, and even the Post Office worker who writes outlines are guilty of succumbing to language when they ought to have mastered it. Mastery over language can never be complete, but only economic—the constant exertion of an amount of energy that is just more than equal to the energy of its opponent. Language is resistant yet submissive; it has the special property, if it is automatically written, of vanishing in the conveyance of meaning. Realistic writing, as Trollope describes it, is the paradoxical feat of balancing the written word in a state of simultaneous presence and absence, necessity and negligibility. And the labor that maintains this balance must also look like ease.

The *Autobiography* offers a series of trite metaphors for writing, all of which refer not to what writing is but to what it can become under the proper treatment. The novelist's writing "must come from him as music comes from the rapid touch of the great performer's fingers; as words come from the mouth of the indignant orator; as letters fly from the fingers of the trained compositor; as the syllables tinkled out by little bells form themselves to the ear of the telegraphist" (152). In all these cases, the skill of transmitting the message is not the same as the skill of composing it. Indeed, the transmitter need not be the same person as the composer. In the novelist's case, transmitter and composer are the same person; but with his usual fondness for self-division, Trollope treats them as if they were two. When he sits down to write, the novelist becomes his own amanuensis. It would be as outrageous for him to write for writing's sake as it would be for the telegraphist to tinkle his little bells because he likes their sound.

For all the inconsistencies and contradictions in Trollope's figures for writing, they do have a consistent rhetorical effect: the removal of writing from sympathy, from meaning, from life, from everything of value in the whole novel business. The worst thing that can happen to a novelist is that he should grow so enervated that he starts writing "because he has to tell a story" and not "because he has a story to tell." It may seem inconsistent that the *Autobiography* should sharply condemn novelists for whom their profession has become "simply a trade," but their sin is not the possession of a mechanical mind or a shoemaker's sensibility. It is that they have put writing first. They have not followed the proper sequence of realistic novel making. For the realistic novelist, "some series of events, or some development of character, will have presented itself to his imagination,—and this he feels so strongly that he thinks he can present his picture in strong and agreeable language to others" (197). Only the written-out realist is likely to reverse the order of conception and writing, but the reversal puts him in company with those others who think that writing can start something—the poet, the sensationalist, the writer of first drafts. Anyone who regards writing as more than an invisible vehicle will fail at the art of the realistic novel.

The
Other Machine

THE EXCLUSION OF writing from reality is the primary mechanism of the Trollopian novel-machine. A number of other exclusions follow from it. The novelist's life is separated from his art, and the novelist himself is divided into two separate faculties, one of which conceives while the other writes down the conception. Realistic writing is set apart from the other kinds of writing that produce poetry and sensationalism. Within the realistic novel, the text is separated from its meaning and plot is separated from character. Trollope makes these operations seem natural and easy, but the performance of them always encounters resistance. Between each pair of opposites is an attraction that must be countered: there is a tendency for the oppositions to collapse, for the values of the terms to reverse themselves. Autobiographers are tempted to speak about themselves, writers are inclined to rewrite, and readers often prefer the unraveling of plot to the elucidation of character. The exclusion can never be complete; one term of the opposition can never simply eliminate the other. Indeed, Trollope's theory never proposes, even as an ideal, such a state of purity. The valuable term in each opposition—conception, realism, meaning, character—is said to be proper or right; it corresponds to the novelist's desire. The worthless term—writing, sensationalism, textuality, plot—is said to be empty or suspect; it is imposed on the novelist by the nature of things, and though he does not like it, he makes do somehow. Making do is the novelist's business, and he is so taken up by it that he never pauses to imagine what his business might be if he had things entirely his own way.

Yet Trollope's theory does contain an image of the ideal novel. It is the time of living-with, when the novelist is engaged in getting to know the characters he has conceived. The whole process, though it involves the duality of a knower and a thing to be known, takes place within the unity of the novelist's mind. There is no opposition here, and no temptation to be resisted. No writing has yet been done, and there is no need for signification of any kind between two terms that are also one. This scene of communion has always already begun, and the eventual writing of a novel neither ends nor alters it. The system is complete as it stands; only the desire to bring readers into it gives rise to the impurities with which the practicing novelist has to deal. But this complete system, this ideal novel, is no novel at all, only a castle in the air. All the impurities in the novel business invade the system when it decides to go public. That decision is not imposed from outside, as the impurities are said to be; it is the system itself that decides that, for all its self-sufficiency, it is incomplete. No external necessity compels young Anthony Trollope to lay his identity aside and become a novelist. Indeed, as the *Autobiography* tells it, nothing could have been less appropriate, less necessary, than this event. But the ideal novel is less than pure even at its origin. It requires the supplement of writing to verify its own purity.

Whenever Trollope's theory sets up an opposition, it attributes great value to one term and little value to the other. None of Trollope's terminology is invented by the theory; all of it is borrowed from tradition and contemporary criticism, and all pairs of opposites are clichés. The theory is distinctively Trollopian only in its assignment of values. It does not define but takes for granted what the components of a novel are, specifying only how those given components are to be regarded if a certain goal is to be achieved. Even that goal is a cliché—that fiction ought to seem real. The realistic novel described by Trollope's theory is a medium of persuasion; the realistic novelist is a rhetorician rather than a representer. Just as Trollope's theory assigns distinctive values to terms that it takes ready-made from the world, so the novels described by the theory teach readers to evaluate what the world already contains. The realistic novel does not create or even imitate a world. Its primary purpose is to teach how the given world is to be looked at. It persuades its reader that certain things are true of the world in which both he and the novel find themselves. The equivalence of fiction and reality, and the exclusion of writing from the relation, might seem to make the novelist anything but a rhetorician, adept in the very thing that has no value and ought to be ignored. But there is no other way to exclude writing from reality than to write the exclusion down: reality is defined by its difference from writing, and the definition is a written one.

According to Trollope, the "reality" that a realistic novel portrays does not transcend the portrayal but adjoins it. This, in Hawthorne's figure of a world under glass, is the relation of the real world to the Trollopian novel—a metonymic rather than a metaphoric relation.[1] The novel world is in no way different from the real world except in its enclosure, its circumscription. Any imitation can be recognized as such by its difference from what it imitates, but in Trollope's theory it is precisely the recognition of this difference that the novelist's labor is intended to suppress. Those things in the novel business that are to be reduced to a minimum are the things that remind the reader (and the novelist) that the novel is writing, not life, and that the novel may point to life but it cannot be identical with it. If the novel is recognized as nothing more than a piece of writing, the values of Trollope's theory reverse themselves: the real world, too, is a piece of writing. The world becomes a sort of text before the book, and the novelist's labor becomes the slicing of the prewritten world into marketable sections. The world and the novel are still identical, but now both are written. One reason, in this view, why novel writing needs to be so tightly controlled is that there is a limitless quantity of world, as there is of ink, and unless the writer restrains himself he will write without limit. One reason, also, why the realistic novelist's every word must be accurate as soon as it appears is that he is neither making up the world nor copying it, but merely measuring the world itself.

If the world is prewritten, then the characters of a future novel are already in writing before the novelist conceives them, and living-with is an act of reading. The reader's achievement of a sympathy exactly equivalent to the novelist's is then another metonymic relation: the reader replaces the novelist by reading exactly the same text—not a substitute or a sign for that text, but the very text that *is* character. The novelist has made the replacement possible by removing his identity from the novel,

[1]The metaphor agrees with Roman Jakobson's theory that it is "the predominance of metonymy which underlies and actually predetermines the so-called 'realistic' trend of mid-nineteenth-century literature" ("Two Aspects of Language and Two Types of Aphasic Disturbances," in Roman Jakobson and Morris Halle, *Fundamentals of Language*, 2nd ed. [The Hague: Mouton, 1971], p. 92).

leaving a place for the reader to fill. The novelist's relation to his characters in the time of living-with is analogous to the reader's relation to the text of a realistic novel. Character is analogous to writing: not only is it inscribed on a surface, but it also has all the permanence and unalterability that any written text presents to a reader who has not written it. The text is always already there, for both novelist and reader; living-with, like reading, makes no change in the text. Though Trollope's theory describes living-with in terms of full human community, it is one sided in a way that resembles reading more than good fellowship. Living-with might better be called living-beside, pressing one's nose against the glass that divides reader and novelist from these living people who do not know that they are "being made a show of." Even before he writes, the novelist gets no closer to his characters than this. His intimacy with them can be duplicated by a reader because it is no closer than the intimacy of any reader with any written text.

To redescribe Trollope's theory in this way is to turn it upside down—to make primary what Trollope calls supplemental and to turn over the whole novel business to what the theory demands be subdued in it. But in Trollope's theory, opposites are always economically inter-related, and the novel-machine runs on the energy of their interrelation, the tension of dualities that are also unities. What Trollope's theory *says* stands in just such a relation to what it *describes*. The theory says that there is a world free of writing that the novelist can know as such and that he can duplicate for the reader by means of a written supplement that exists only to efface itself. The theory describes the opposite of this: a world made entirely of writing, which can be given directly to the reader in its exact and only form because it has never been anything but the world text that the novelist first reads and then cuts into pieces, as Hawthorne's giant hews out his "lump of earth." These two worlds exist only in their difference from each other; the realistic novel requires the opposite of realism in order to define itself.

The sensation novel, in Trollope's account of it, contains all the properties of the novel that realism ought to minimize in itself: "sensation novel" is the name that the novel-machine gives to its own mirror image. But the sensation novel was also a real-life phenomenon, an event in the insignificant life of Anthony Trollope. Trollope's theory did not and does not exist in isolation from the real-life circumstances of its writing. Sometimes it conforms to the mid-Victorian commonplace, sometimes it diverges significantly from the common. But always, and particularly in the case of the sensation novel, Trollope's theory can best be understood

as working in shifting, dynamic relation to the clichés of his contemporaries. There is also clear evidence, in many of Trollope's novels, of a
tendency to imitate his theoretical opponents, to adopt from them themes,
subjects, and methods that would never appear there if theory were the
master of practice. The relation between Trollope and the sensationalists
was much closer and much more complex than the *Autobiography* admits;
the theoretical opposite of realism was not external to realism but its
inseparable companion.

The literary background of the sensation novel has been examined
elsewhere.[2] Nothing about the genre was new; its heritage included Scott,
Godwin, Mrs. Radcliffe, and even Shakespeare. The terms "sensation"
and "sensational," however, were new to literary criticism in the 1860s.
Like "realism," and following it by a few years, "sensationalism" was
adopted by literary critics to designate what was thought of as a new
subcategory of novels.[3] The advent of the term "sensation" in the English
critical vocabulary can be fairly precisely dated: it was first applied to
Dion Boucicault's *The Colleen Bawn*, which opened at the Adelphi in
September 1860.[4] The success of this play, in company with the even
greater success of *The Woman in White* (which had completed serial
publication in August of the same year), convinced literary critics that a
new kind of writing had been born and that, as Margaret Oliphant
declared, "the universal verdict" had "crowned it with success."[5]

One can hardly estimate the effect of this phenomenon on Trollope,

[2]Walter C. Phillips, *Dickens, Reade, and Collins, Sensation Novelists: A Study in the
Conditions and Theories of Novel Writing in Victorian England* (New York: Columbia
University Press, 1919).

[3]When Henry Trollope assigned headings to the right-hand pages of the *Autobiography*
(xvii), he chose "Realism and Sensationalism" to head his father's discussion of the subject.
Trollope himself, however, uses only "realistic" and "sensational," never attributing to
either mode of writing the ideological suffix -ism. In *Thackeray*, "realism" is a matter of
style, particularly dialogue; it is a middle style, bordered on either side by the "sublime" and
the "ludicrous" (pp. 181-82). The *OED* cites as the earliest use of "sensationalism" in a
literary context the review of J. S. LeFanu's *Uncle Silas* in the *Saturday Review* 19
(4 February 1865): 145. "Sensation" was used in a similar sense, however, at least four years
earlier, and "sensational" quickly followed it. In this case and others, Trollope's vocabulary
and opinions are centered in the early and middle 1860s, the time of his own greatest
popular success. Much of what the *Autobiography* takes for granted as current was ten
years out of date when the book was written, and closer to twenty when it was published.

[4]The earliest usage I have found of this term is in "The New Sensation-Drama," *Spectator*
34 (23 November 1861): 1284. It was evidently common before that date, however, because
a month later, in "The Enigma Novel," *Spectator* 34 (28 December 1861): 1428, Frances
Browne's *The Castleford Case* is already greeted as "a new species of the sensation novel."
Later critics sometimes cite *The Colleen Bawn* as the origin of sensation, as, for example,
the author of "The Theatres," *Saturday Review* 26 (26 September 1868): 427, who remarks
that "since the *Colleen Bawn* gave rise to the expression 'sensational,' the word has undergone
a considerable modification."

[5]"Sensation Novels," *Blackwood's* 111 (May 1862): 565.

whose own "First Success," as the *Autobiography* calls it, had been *The Warden* in 1855, and whose first great financial and popular success was *Framley Parsonage*, which concluded publication in the *Cornhill* in the spring of 1861. In the early 1860s, Trollope's realism shared the novel market with the sensationalism of his opponents. While Trollope was expanding Barsetshire and inaugurating the Palliser series with *The Small House at Allington* and *Can You Forgive Her?* (1864), Wilkie Collins was winning equal fame and more money with *No Name* (1863) and *Armadale* (1866). Trollope, along with many contemporary critics, always treats the sensation novel as an upstart, a modern deviance from the tradition of Jane Austen and Walter Scott that Trollope's novels continue. But for the reading public, the market whose demands Trollope is always eager to meet, the sensation novel and the Trollopian novel were parallel phenomena, rising into success within the same few years and falling together into disfavor by the mid-1870s.

After *The Way We Live Now* (1875), Trollope encountered the "diminution in price" that the *Autobiography* records in a footnote (138), and by that date critics were generally agreed that the sensation novel, having reached "the full measure of its absurdity" in fifteen years, stood at the end of its career.[6] It had been a critical commonplace that Trollope was the preeminent "non-sensational writer," as the *Autobiography* admits,[7] and this distinction outlived the heyday of both kinds of writing. But the new novelists of the 1870s were not considered to have returned to the Trollopian norm; rather, they lumped Trollope and the sensationalists together and rejected both. As Swinburne wrote in 1876, commenting on the murkiness of Meredith's new novel, *Beauchamp's Career:* "By dint of revulsion from Trollope on this hand and Braddon on that, he seems to have persuaded himself that limpidity of style must mean shallowness, lucidity of narrative must imply triviality, and simplicity of direct interest or positive incident must involve 'sensationalism.'"[8] According to Trollope's theory, realism is the opposite of sensationalism and its far superior; but the reading public was able to treat both kinds of writing as equal and to welcome a third kind when it seemed to present itself.

The discussion of sensationalism in the *Autobiography* is an expanded and slightly revised version (many whole sentences are unchanged) of

[6]Review of *The Mystery of Ashleigh Manor*, *Saturday Review* 37 (25 April 1874): 539.

[7]For example, the review of *Lotta Schmidt and Other Stories*, *Saturday Review* 24 (21 December 1867): 381.

[8]Letter to John Morley, in Cecil Y. Lang, ed., *The Swinburne Letters*, 6 vols. (New Haven: Yale University Press, 1959-62), 3: 131.

remarks made in Trollope's lecture "On English Prose Fiction as a Rational Amusement," prepared in 1870. The same passage, vitually unaltered, appears in the essay "Novel-Reading," published in 1879. Trollope's first statement on sensationalism, in which most of the same points are made, was a response to Archbishop Thomson, the outspoken critic of sensationalism from whom I have quoted in chapter 3. Having read in *The Times* about the archbishop's notorious speech at Huddersfield, Trollope wrote to his publisher, George Smith, proposing to write a short article to refute the archbishop's claims. "His object was to answer the attack made on sensationalists by showing that all modern English novels present life decently and do little or no harm; that, indeed, they do good, taking poetry's place in cultivating the imagination; that they advocate those lessons of life which mammas teach, or ought to teach, to their daughters."[9] Smith, perhaps feeling that Archbishop Thomson had been refuted often enough, discouraged the project, and the article was never written. But the proposal stuck with Trollope, and many of its contentions appear unchanged in texts of 1870, 1875, and 1879.

Like the other elements of Trollope's theory, his opinion of the sensation novel does not change from one exposition of it to the next. It is perhaps a surprising opinion, given the radical difference of Trollope's fictional practice from that of Wilkie Collins or Miss Braddon. Trollope neither attacks nor denigrates sensationalism; rather, he tries to break down the distinction that would make "sensation" the property of only a certain kind of novel and to claim that it belongs to all good novels, including his own. He begins by attacking the "great division" that is made among contemporary novels, novelists, and novel readers, separating them into sensational and antisensational camps. Antisensational novelists, according to Trollope, "are generally called realistic"; Wilkie Collins is sensational, while "I am realistic." Sensational readers enjoy "the construction and gradual development of a plot"; antisensational readers prefer "the elucidation of character." This is a reasonably accurate description of critical terms that were in vogue during the 1860s and 70s, though Trollope makes the oppositions much sharper than any other commentator did. Sensation novels and novelists were recognized as special types, but no one else went so far as to identify a class of sensation readers, too. No one else called the opposite of Collins and Braddon "antisensational," as if there were some ideological antagonism between the two parties, or as if the antisensationalists could be recognized only

---

[9]Letter to George Smith, 4 November 1864, in Bradford A. Booth, ed., *The Letters of Anthony Trollope* (London: Oxford University Press, 1951), p. 159. I quote Booth's paraphrase.

by their difference from a sensational standard. But then Trollope de-molishes his own distinction by calling it "a mistake" (194).

Both the distinction and its demolition are elements in Trollope's theory much more than they are events in the world of mid-Victorian literature. As I have shown, the theory regards the stimulation of sym-pathy as the primary aim of all novelists and novels. Sympathy links the reader to the novelist by recreating the experience of living-with, and it teaches the reader how to look at his world. Sympathy can be felt only for characters; they are the most important elements in the process of conceiving, writing, and reading novels. It is a threat to the supremacy of Trollopian realism that there should exist an alternative machine founded on the exploitation of plot rather than character, writing rather than sympathy. The existence of such a machine must be "a mistake": the hypothetical sensation novel is described by the *Autobiography* as in every way external to Trollopian realism, but in fact the rival machine is the negative image of Trollopian realism itself.

Trollope explains the mistake away by demonstrating that realism and sensationalism are not opposed: only the "imperfect artist" makes them seem to be. A "good" novel is both realistic and sensational "in the highest degree," and if a novel is not so "there is a failure in art" (194). In the argument that follows, some clever rhetorical sleight of hand goes to work. "Sensational scenes" are first described as those in any novel that elicit the strongest response; then such response is declared to be impos-sible in a novel peopled by "personages without character,—wooden blocks, who cannot make themselves known to the reader as men and women" (195). It is concluded that, if a novel contains "truth of character, truth as to men and women," it can never be "too sensational" (196). The result of this rather devious logic is that the primacy of plot, which is said at first to be distinctive of sensation novels, turns out to be distinctive only of bad novels. Good novels are still Trollope's own kind; good sensationalism is the same as realism.

I have dwelt so long on this apparently minor passage in the *Auto-biography* because it is the clearest case of Trollope's encounter with his self-made opposite. The argument for/against sensationalism is a set piece: formulated as early as 1864, it found its way with very little change into a survey of the English novel in 1870, the *Autobiography* in 1875-76, and a review of collected editions of Dickens and Thackeray in 1879. Any context was right for it, and no number of repetitions could spoil the neatness with which it explains away all dangers. It is also a dis-ingenuous performance from a writer whose rhetoric is usually supposed to be nonexistent. It does not mirror the real world accurately, nor do its conclusions follow from its premises, but this is not because Trollope misunderstood sensationalism or because he was incapable of logical thinking. Rather, as the passage itself makes clear, realism includes its own opposite and also demands that its opposite be excluded.

For mid-Victorian critics, it was precisely the element in sensationalism that Trollope finesses—its foundation in plot rather than character —that distinguished it from all other kinds of fiction. This difference prevented any sensation novel from attaining the first rank of excellence, but it did suffice to identify such novels as a special category, an identification that Trollope seeks to efface. At this point "sensationalism" takes leave of the current events from which it is ostensibly drawn and installs itself as an element in Trollope's theory, irrespective of what the world was actually reading. Starting when the sensation novel was at its peak of notoriety in the early 1860s and continuing throughout his career, Trollope repeatedly imitated his upstart opponents—though there is no evidence that they ever imitated him. Of course, if one follows Trollope's theory, reality itself is the stuff of his fiction, not some stylish or idiosyncratic version of it; so that any novel that at all attempts to imitate life would be imitating Trollope. But there are particular features of life —primarily elements of plot—that were recognized as distinctively "sensational," and though they are of no importance in Trollope's fiction before the 1860s, they enter it then and recur in it frequently thereafter.

The first instance of Trollopian sensationalism is *Orley Farm* (1862), whose plot, according to the *Autobiography*, is "probably the best I have ever made" (143). The resemblance of this plot to those of the sensationalists is more than incidental; it is blatant. The resemblance was noted by Alexander Smith in an ambitious article for the *North British Review* of 1863. In Smith's opinion, the unlikely trio of *No Name*, *Lady Audley's Secret*, and *Orley Farm* all fostered the same "morbid condition in the public mind."[10] For Trollope's first biographer, T.H.S. Escott, the kinship was equally clear, and its cause was obvious:

> During the early sixties the popularity of the sensation novel . . . was confirmed by Wilkie Collins and was still further increased and extended by Miss Braddon. No one . . . mirrored more promptly and faithfully than Trollope the literary tendencies of this time. Always quick to take a hint, Trollope therefore introduced the sensational element into the novel *Orley Farm*, and by its successful appeal to interests, which it had not yet fallen within his scope to touch, competely justified the new experiment.[11]

[10]"Novels and Novelists of the Day," *North British Review* 38 (February 1863): 188.
[11]*Anthony Trollope: His Work, Associates, and Literary Originals* (London: John Lane, 1913), p. 188.

This significant observation—which, like most of Escott's observations, has all the novelty of a fifty-year-old cliché—has been made again by subsequent critics in regard to specific cases of resemblance.[12]

The similarity of some of Trollope's novels to those of his sensational adversaries, and even the fact that the similarity is more likely intended than accidental, is less significant than the way in which the would-be sensational features of Trollope's fiction are treated by the fiction itself. The theory always excludes sensation: the *Autobiography* goes so far as to list *Orley Farm* with *Ivanhoe, Old Mortality, Jane Eyre,* and *Henry Esmond* among novels whose authors have not "sinned in being over-sensational" (195). It is true that *Orley Farm* cannot be accused of being more than half-sensational. For almost precisely half its length, it toys with the mystery of whether Lady Mason forged her husband's will, but at the midpoint the mystery is suddenly resolved—saving the novel from the charge of outright sensationalism, but also giving its plot "the fault of declaring itself, and thus coming to an end too early in the book" (143). The novel draws attention to its own default. At the end of chapter 44, Lady Mason sensationally declares that she is "guilty of all this with which they charge me." But chapter 45 begins: "I venture to think, I may almost say to hope, that Lady Mason's confession at the end of the last chapter will not have taken anybody by surprise. If such surprises be felt I must have told my tale badly. I do not like such revulsions of feeling with regard to my characters as surprises of this nature must generate." For its first half, *Orley Farm* has been as mysterious about Lady Mason's guilt as any sensation novel could have been, and it has even provided a sensational revelation of the truth. But if the reader was surprised, he is immediately told that he has made a mistake. The novel is not sensational, and only incorrect reading makes it seem so. Again, as in the theory, sensationalism has been included and excluded at once, exploited and then denied.

[12]In *"The Eustace Diamonds* and *The Moonstone," Studies in Philology* 36 (1939): 651-63, Henry J. W. Milley was the first modern critic to do so, making a convincing case that Trollope's novel can be read as a parody of Collins's. Recently, Norman Donaldson, in his introduction to a reprint of *The Claverings* (New York: Dover, 1977), has noted some plausible resemblances between that novel and *Uncle Silas.* The fullest consideration of Trollope's "imitation" of the sensationalists, however, remains Bradford A. Booth's *"Orley Farm:* Artistry *Manqué,"* in *From Jane Austen to Joseph Conrad: Essays Collected in Honor of James T. Hillhouse* (Minneapolis: University of Minnesota Press, 1958), pp. 146-59. Booth notes that *Orley Farm* appeared when "the Victorian sensation novel was sweeping all before it," and that *Doctor Thorne* comes "perilously close to giving way to sensationalism" (p. 146). He adds, however, that neither those novels nor their vaguely sensational successors like *The Last Chronicle of Barset* can be called truly sensational, because none has its *"raison d'être* in the solving of a mystery" (p. 147). Booth concludes, with Trollope, that Trollope is "a realist and anti-sensationalist" (p. 149).

Similar strategies are employed whenever the style or the subjects of Trollope's later novels verge on what a reader of the 1860s would recognize as "sensationalism." Even as late as *Doctor Wortle's School*, which was written (1879) and published (1881) long after the fad for sensation had faded, half a chapter is devoted to declaring that the storyteller has decided "to depart altogether from those principles of storytelling to which you probably have become accustomed." He unravels the mystery at length and concludes with the warning that "they who feel that on this account all hope of interest is at an end had better put down the book." His unraveling, however, is an elaborate begging of the question, since it goes no further than to state that Mrs. Peacocke "was a bigamist,—that is, if any second marriage had ever been perpetrated." The latter mystification is sustained until chapter 7, and the whole mystery is not cleared up until chapter 10 of the second volume —exactly the "last chapter but two" that is cited as the proper place for any novel but this one to make its revelations (3). In both technique and subject, *Doctor Wortle's School* is a full-fledged sensation novel written fifteen years too late. It is a tour de force of a particularly obscure kind, the simultaneous exploitation and demolition of an opponent that, by the time the novel was written, had lost its power in the real world while entrenching itself all the more firmly within the Trollopian novel-machine.[13]

In Trollope's theory, "sensationalism" involves a good deal more than the employment of topics like bigamy and murder. It stands for any kind of writing that surrenders to the temptations of writing itself, bypassing the multiple restrictions that Trollope places on that tempting activity. Prominent among the temptations is the urge to keep secrets from the reader. Wilkie Collins and Miss Braddon were famous for their skill at keeping secrets, and the examples I have cited show Trollope keeping them with equal skill but denying it. As early as *Barchester Towers*, however, long before the sensational had been defined as a category of novels, Trollope was declaring himself opposed to "that system which goes so far as to violate all proper confidence between the author and his readers, by maintaining nearly to the end of the third volume a mystery as to the fate of their favourite personage": "Our doctrine is that the author and the reader should move along together, in

[13]Sensational topics and techniques appear frequently in Trollope's novels after *Orley Farm*, always accompanied by some sort of denial that they are what they seem. It may help to account for the decline in Trollope's reputation in the last years of his life that he remained concerned with the appropriation of matters that had once defined his opponents, but that by that time had lost their significance for everyone but Trollope himself.

full confidence with each other. Let the personages of the drama undergo ever so complete a comedy of errors among themselves, but let the spectator never mistake the Syracusan for the Ephesian; otherwise, he is one of the dupes, and the part of a dupe is never dignified" (15).

A similar declaration is made in *The Eustace Diamonds*—"He who recounts these details has scorned to have a secret between himself and his readers" (48)—and it becomes a challenge in the passage from *Doctor Wortle's School* that I have quoted. Such statements invite the reader to believe that he is repeating the writing of the novel, just as in the *Autobiography* writing repeats the reading of character that has preceded it. If both novelist and reader maintain this belief, it will bring them closer —indeed, it will merge them. But whatever comfort may derive from such imagined identity is won only by evading a fact about writing: the writer was always there first, and the medium that brings him into his readers' company also separates him absolutely from them.

Trollope's theory requires that the novelist's identity or self-personality be absent from his novels, removed from them by an act of will. Sensationalism, poetry, and plot, along with the writing of any first draft, have in common that they assert the personality of the writer, while Trollopian realism always suppresses it. Whatever storyteller the reader of a Trollope novel may feel close to, therefore, cannot be Trollope himself. The storyteller is generated by the reader's encounter with the text; he is a sort of phantom figure, like the ghost who writes the *Autobiography.* Again, though Trollope's theory says that it deals primarily in things that are not written, everything the theory describes is writing in different guises, different written figures. Trollopian realism puts constant pressure on writing to look like anything but itself. Writing always has a degree of mystification in it, since the writer has already written every word before the reader reads it. But this insincerity can be consigned to plot, the smallest possible part of a realistic novel, because if it is restricted there, the rest of the novel must be sincere. This is what happens in *Orley Farm*: its plot "comes to an end" halfway through the book, leaving the rest to character and sympathy. The same is true of the other aspects of writing—linearity, sequentiality, signification—that are included in plot but excluded from the rest of the novel. Their partial presence assures the presence of what is different from them. In this way, Trollope's realism depends upon the things that it claims have been forced on it from outside. The novel can never be a pure art form, because its valuable components can exist only in their difference from its worthless ones.

Trollope's objections to the excesses of the sensation novel seem to be moral and esthetic: "Horrors heaped upon horrors, and which are horrors only in themselves, and not as touching any recognised and known person, are not tragic, and soon cease even to horrify." As the objections continue, however, and as Trollope provides his own sensation novel in miniature, the danger of sensationalism shows itself in different terms: "And such would-be tragic elements of a story may be increased without end, and without difficulty. I may tell you of a woman murdered,—murdered in the same street with you, in the next house,—that she was a wife murdered by her husband,—a bride not yet a week a wife. I may add to it for ever. I may say that the murderer roasted her alive. There is no end to it" (195). Without the limitation of character, which binds writing to the equivalent realities that precede and follow it, there would indeed be no end to writing. The reason for the exclusion of such "would-be tragic elements" is not that they are immoral but that "there is nothing so easy as the creation and the cumulation of fearful incidents after this fashion." Few writers would agree that such things are easy, or at least that ease should make one avoid them. But in the language of Trollope's theory, ease is temptation and temptation is danger—the danger of writing itself, which without the real world to control it would know no limits.

The realistic novel, as Trollope's theory describes it, is a system of writing that pushes in two opposed directions and whose enforced equilibrium makes a work of art. One kind of writing, called plot, pushes toward the limitless proliferation of writing itself. The other kind, called character, pushes inward, restraining writing within the limits of correspondence to the real world. The theory assigns all value to this unwritten writing of character, withholding value from any writing that admits its nature—and from all writers, like poets and sensation novelists, who surrender to the temptation of words. But the theory contains its own opposite: what the theory describes—the opposite of what it says—is a state in which writing was always there first, producing everything that is said to be other than itself. The world is writing; the novelist writes the world. The novelist, indeed, makes the world exist by writing it, and he makes himself exist the same way. The novel-machine keeps running because no permanent balance can ever be maintained between the boundless desire to write and the equal desire to be writing *about* something.

But the desire to write precedes the desire to have a subject—just the condition of those tired novelists for whom their work has become "simply a trade" (197). Trollope was never tired, but he was forming "plays" within himself before he joined the world. And toward the end of his life, as his audience shrank and unpublished novels piled up, he began to acknowledge the primacy of what had always been his first desire. As he wrote to his son in 1880: "I finished on Thursday the novel I was writing, and on Friday I began another. Nothing really frightens me but the idea of enforced idleness. As long as I can write books, even though they be not published, I think that I can be happy."[14] In the end, Trollope's life took on, like his theory, the character of what it intended to exclude—a voluminous outpouring of writing that exceeded the existence of the man who had worked all his life to restrain it.

[14]Letter to Henry Trollope, 21 December 1880, *Letters*, p. 446.

The Rhetoric of Reality

IN THE *AUTOBIOGRAPHY*, "the novelist" is interchangeable with Anthony Trollope, and all "good novels" are as much as possible like Trollope's own. The theory propounded in the *Autobiography* is a design for reading as much as for writing, and the most appropriate novels to read in the Trollopian way would be the novels Trollope wrote. To read in the Trollopian way is easy, so easy that it seems natural; Trollope's theory instructs us with great care to do what we already know how to do uninstructed. The *Autobiography* has never been regarded as a theoretical text, and its first readers were embarrassed and offended by it—largely because it seems to say nothing new and to do so with an air of unsophisticated self-satisfaction.

But the *Autobiography* is, if anything, oversophisticated, and the perpetual-motion machine it describes is kept moving by the impossibility that its desire will ever be satisfied. Trollope's theory is an elaborate exercise in a very subtle rhetoric, persuading its reader that certain things are true about fiction. The theory describes realistic novels as equally elaborate exercises in an equally subtle rhetoric, persuading their readers that certain things are true about life. And the most important of these things is that good fiction (Trollope's) is equivalent to life (all life). To read Trollope's novels in the Trollopian way means nothing more demanding than to accept them as stories about real people. But if the rhetoric of fiction is the rhetoric of reality, then the strategies of reading are the same as those of living, and a novel about real people is just as much about realistic novels. Here and there in the preceding chapters, I have called upon the novels to elucidate one point or another in the theory. In this and the following chapters, I will do the reverse, employing the theory to elucidate the novels. Neither is subordinate to or parasitic on the other: theory is a translation of practice, and practice is a translation of theory.

I will read Trollope's novels topically, cutting them up into categories that are derived from the theory but that the novels themselves do not acknowledge. The theory says that Trollope's novels are a continuous dispensing of a continuous reality; all subdivisions in this continuum, even when they are necessary, ought to be ignored. Though each Trollope novel does have its own structure—a matter that I will discuss in chapter 7—the continuity of the world represented in all the novels, and the equal continuity of the reader's sympathy with that world, is more important than the structure of any single work. To this degree, my reading of Trollope's novels will be authorized by his theory. But my reading will disobey the theory in that I will also ignore the lines that separate one character from another, and even the difference between the characters and their narrator. The moral values attributed to the characters are, of course, important; and these are related to the context in which each character is written. Whether a character is good, bad, or doubtful, whether he finds himself in a situation of joy or sorrow, ease or stress—all these things help to determine the value of what he says and what the narrator says about him. But the topics I will treat have a double reference: to their particular context (the nature of the character or situation with which they are connected) and to their general context (the promulgation by the novels of a plan for reading realistically). My concern will be primarily with the latter reference, and it requires an anti-Trollopian approach to Trollope—reading his characters as rhetorical strategies rather than as living people seen through writing.

In the *Autobiography*, realistic fiction is distinguished from all other kinds of writing by a fundamental difference in the way language is used by them. The nonrealistic writer labors self-consciously over his language. He thereby exalts himself unduly, soaring into the skies like a bulky sylph and dragging his readers after him into a zone peopled by "gods or demons" with whom no one can sympathize (125). The realistic reader gets only a bad taste or smell from such writing, but there are nonrealistic readers who get an unaccountable pleasure from this pointless exercise and who are willing to let themselves be carried away wherever the soaring writer may take them. In the novels, "poetry," "romance," and other related terms are applied to ways of living or looking at the world, not primarily to ways of writing or reading. But the same negative values are attached to them in the novels as the *Autobiography* gives them in a specifically literary context. Trollope's novels and his theory define their territory in the same way, by excluding their literary opposites; and in the novels there is just as much allure to what is excluded as there is in the theory. Trollope's characters define their lives as the theory defines his fiction. In both cases, the definition of a proper territory is also the definition of an improper one, which must be contained or excluded. In the novels, however, literary terms have little overtly literary reference, because to the eye of the realist, there is (or ought to be) no difference between literature and life.

The most prominent literary terms that the novels use in nonliterary ways are "poetry" and "poetical." Poems are uncommon in Trollope's novels. Trollope's prose is uninterrupted by poetry, except for a tag or a jingle now and then, and in the world of his characters, poems appear mainly as articles of drawing room furniture, diversions for an idle moment. Poems may also be used for unsavory purposes, as in *The Prime Minister* by the specious Ferdinand Lopez, who wins Emily Wharton's heart with loose talk of "books,—and especially of poetry" (44). Practicing poets are rare in Trollope's novels. One of them narrowly misses attending Melmotte's disastrous dinner in *The Way We Live Now* (59), but the most prominent example is the "Republican Browning," the absurd Wallachia Petrie of *He Knew He Was Right*, who has composed her "well-known piece" entitled "Ancient Marbles, while ye crumble" in expression of nothing more high flown than resentment of the aristocratic Mr. Glascock (55). Some of Trollope's unsteadier characters, like Johnny Eames in *The Small House at Allington* (4) and Louis Trevelyan in *He Knew He Was Right* (1), have composed poetry in their youth. Most of them, however, recover from the habit (if not the tendency) in their later life.

Like his contemporaries, Trollope makes poetry more a matter of vision and feeling than of metrics.[1] The "poetical" in his novels has little explicitly to do with poems. It is often associated with certain kinds of scenery, and with the feelings such scenes inspire in the characters who look at them. Moonlight and mountains are poetical, as are the seashore and any rocky vista. Amid the ruins of Matching Priory in *Can You*

---

[1]See A. H. Warren, *English Poetic Theory, 1825-1865* (Princeton: Princeton University Press, 1950), p. 29.

Forgive Her? Lady Glencora gets the poetical feeling:

> 'Is it not beautiful!' said Glencora. 'I do love it so! And there is a peculiar feeling of cold about the chill of the moon, different from any other cold. It makes you wrap yourself up tight, but it does not make your teeth chatter; and it seems to go into your senses rather than into your bones. But I suppose that's nonsense,' she added after a pause.
> 'Not more so than what people are supposed to talk by moonlight.'
> 'That's unkind. I'd like what I say on such an occasion to be more poetical or else more nonsensical than what other people say under the same circumstances.' (27)

Because she understands the link between poetry and nonsense (or their identity), Glencora can safely indulge in a bout of poetical feelings without real danger of being "carried away" among gods or demons. Her booklength flirtation with Burgo Fitzgerald, indulged in for a while and then terminated by the assertion of common sense over nonsense, has the same structure as this little scene, and both have the same outcome—the choice of the real instead of the poetical.

Lizzie Eustace faces a similar choice in *The Eustace Diamonds*, but because Lizzie is "stupidly unacquainted with circumstances, and a liar at the same time" (10), she always chooses wrongly. Lizie's venal ignorance is associated not only with poetical scenes but also with poems, chiefly Romantic poems. One of the most malicious scenes in this eminently malicious novel offers the spectacle of Lizzie's expedition to the rocky shore, determined to savor *Queen Mab* away from the "coarse, inappropriate, everyday surroundings of the drawing-room." After overcoming the unpoetical obstacles of the hot sun, the narrow bench on which she must sit, and "some snails which discomposed her," she launches into Shelley, at once finding a delightful "antithesis" in the phrase "naked purity." Finally, puffed up with poetry, she rises from the bench, "almost forgetting the heat": "What a tawdry world was this, in which clothes and food and houses are necessary! How perfectly that boy-poet had understood it all! 'Immortal amid ruin!' She liked the idea of the ruin almost as well as that of the immortality, and the stains quite as well as the purity" (21). Lizzie is in danger of being carried away, not only from common sense but altogether out of the real world.

Shelley is not directly responsible for Lizzie's misreading of him, nor for her attempts to apply to real life what was never intended for such application. Yet the nonsense into which Lizzie falls is not entirely of her own making. Shelley's words have a power distinct from their meaning —they are "of a nature which would enable her to remember them"—and their meaning is so badly conveyed by them that she "may be excused for not understanding" what they mean. Glencora's advantage over Lizzie is that Glencora knows how to confine the poetical within certain limits of time and place. Within these limits, poetry is permissible as a mild vacation from the real, because it is innocuous if it is restrained there. Poetry itself does not supply these restraints; they must be imposed by an extrapoetical, realistic intelligence that knows where poetry belongs and can keep it there. Poetry is not competent to teach one about life, nor even to embellish much of it. But poetry is dangerous to ignorant readers like Lizzie, because it does not inform them of its incompetence. Lizzie reads Shelley as if he were Trollope; but this is a natural way to read, and Lizzie is not to blame. The reader of *The Eustace Diamonds* may safely read this way; the novel is fully competent to life, including Shelley, his reading and misreading, and all the aspects of reality with which Shelley has and can have nothing to do. Trollope's fiction claims here what his theory also claims for it—the power to put poetry in its place.

Even worse than by Shelley, Lizzie is misled by Byron. She has read *The Corsair*, and the poem has given her a notion of what love ought to be: "'Ah,' she would say to herself in her moments of solitude, 'if I had a Corsair of my own, how I would sit on watch for my lover's boat by the sea-shore!' And she believed it of herself, that she could do so" (5). For most of the novel, Lizzie searches for a man whom she can cast in the role of Conrad, so that she can play Medora. Lord George is the most promising candidate, but even he, under the pressure of real-life circumstances, collapses eventually from a Corsair into a "brute" (64). At the end, Lizzie marries the "cad" and "Bohemian Jew" Mr. Emilius (80), the farthest possible extreme from a Corsair. The real has turned out to be nor merely different from the poetical, but its opposite. This is a more serious misunderstanding of poetry than the case of *Queen Mab*, because here poetry precedes experience, seems to predict it, and leads Lizzie on a course that only pain and degradation can show to have nothing whatever in common with real life. Again, Lizzie reads poetry as if it were a realistic novel: such novels are supposed to teach girls "what they are to expect when lovers come" (*Autobiography*, 188-89). It is a powerful indictment of poetry that, in the novels, whenever a character attempts to use poetry as a guide to real behavior, the attempt ends in the discovery that only the opposite of poetry is real. It is an even more powerful assertion of the universal competence of realism that it includes both poetry and the junking of it.

Lizzie's case is unusual in Trollope, because her poetical feelings are explicitly connected to the reading of poetry, even specific poems. More often, as in the case of Lady Glencora, poetical feelings are inspired by scenes and situations in the world, not by writing. Yet these scenes and situations are always those that nonrealistic writing has claimed for its own. Poetry is not alone in its attachment to such things; it is often paired with another literary category, also invoked as if it had nothing to do with literature—"romance." The two are frequently linked as equal synonyms for nonsense. "People go on quarrelling and fancying this and that," explains the older, chastened Glencora of *Phineas Redux:*

> and thinking that the world is full of romance and poetry. When they get married they know better.'
>   'I hope the romance and poetry do not all vanish.'
>   'Romance and poetry are for the most part lies, Mr. Maule, and are very apt to bring people into difficulty. I have seen something of them in my time, and I much prefer downright honest figures. Two and two make four; idleness is the root of all evil; love your neighbour like yourself, and the rest of it.' (76)

These are not the figures of poetry, those flights of language that stink of oil and self-aggrandizement. They are clichés, the kind of figures that the *Autobiography* drags out when it wants to show that Trollope is unburdened by genius.[2] They are language used automatically, and therefore truly; no poetical self-personality can claim them for its own.

"Romance," more often than "poetry," is used in Trollope's novels to mean simply nonsense or feeblemindedness. "The belief is theoretic," remarks Plantagenet Palliser in *Phineas Redux*, "or not even quite that. It is hardly more than romantic" (13). "Diamonds are diamonds, and garnets are garnets," says Glencora near the end of *Can You Forgive Her?* "and I am not so romantic but what I know the difference" (79). "Romance" has been used since the fifteenth century to mean a belief or story unrelated to reality, but for Trollope and his contemporaries it was still a literary genre, and a current one. The difference between the romance and the novel was a subject of critical debate well into the 1870s. In 1875, R. H. Hutton devoted much of his review of Mrs. Cashel Hoey's *Blossoming of an Aloe* to showing why the book ought to be praised as a romance, though it might fail as a novel.[3] Most critics agreed with J. C. Jeaffreson's claim, in 1858, that "the distinction that once existed between *novels* and *romances* has for a long time been lost sight of,"[4] or with David Masson's judgment, in 1859, that the distinction "is one more of popular con-

---

[2]Even in a list of clichés, Trollope's rhetoric can demonstrate its idiosyncracies, if not its genius. "Love of money," not idleness, is the "root of all evil," according to Paul's First Epistle to Timothy, 6:10.

[3]*Spectator* 48 (2 January 1875): 18.

[4]*Novels and Novelists from Elizabeth to Victoria*, 2 vols. (London: Hurst & Blackett, 1858), 1: 1.

venience than of inevitable fitness."[5] The terms had even less precision than the generally imprecise vocabulary of mid-Victorian criticism, but when they were distinguished the basis was most often that , in Jeaffreson's terms, the "chief merit" of the romance lay in "the incredibility of its incidents and the wildness of its plot," while the novel adhered to "the simple, and sometimes stern truth of life."[6] Some novelists blurred the distinction by laying claim to both merits in the same work. Charles Reade subtitled his *Hard Cash* (1863) *A Matter-of-Fact Romance*, a combination that one critic found to be "a contradiction in terms."[7] The contradiction was a common one among the sensationalists: James Payn, for example, located his *Found Dead* in "that region of flesh and blood romance, which they who have read little of the book of man denominate the Sensational."

The romance was generally thought of as a more primitive genre than the novel, and the latter was often said to have developed from the former by a process like growing up. Romance had the same archaic aura that surrounded poetry; the novel was for most critics, as it was for Trollope, the distinctively modern genre of fictional writing. Those writers, chiefly the sensationalists, who sought to revitalize romance did so by adding the assurance that a romance could also have some relevance to contemporary life. But "romance" had a long tradition, which made it a more respectable title than the pejorative "sensation novel." J. S. LeFanu, in the "Preliminary Word" to *Uncle Silas*, denies that this "degrading term" is appropriate to his novel, which belongs instead to "the legitimate school of tragic English romance" founded by Walter Scott. For most critics, however, Scott's was too venerable a name to be attached, even as a forebear, to sensationalism. In the *Autobiography*, Trollope includes two scenes from Scott's novels in his list of passages that might seem sensational but really are not (195). And R. H. Hutton refuted LeFanu's claim to kinship with Scott on the grounds that, though there are wild doings in *Ivanhoe*, "no one would call Scott's great romance 'sensational,'" because "the remoteness of the time protects it from the charge."[8] The debate over the difference between novels and romances had more to do with the assignment of values than with the description of literary genres. The romance was older, more primitive, and less pertinent to daily life than the novel, but it had a respectable heritage. Sensation novelists claimed the title, and critics denied it to them, chiefly for reasons of respectability.

[5]*British Novelists and Their Styles* (Boston: Gould & Lincoln, 1859), p. 36.
[6]*Novels and Novelists*, 1: 2.
[7]Edward Dicey, review of *Hard Cash*, *The Reader* 2 (26 December 1863): 753.
[8]"Sensation Novels," *Spectator* 41 (8 August 1868): 932.

The repeated dismissal of "poetry" and "romance" in Trollope's novels implies a literary stance as well as a commonsensical one. The two terms are interchangeable because both refer to that which is extravagant, regressive, irrelevant to life. They are synonyms for nonsense because they seek no equivalence between imagination and reality, the only source of sense for a realist. Both name kinds of feeling that are also kinds of writing, and both are lapses in the lives of Trollope's characters, as they are impurities in the economy of Trollope's theory. The theory, however, does not simply exclude writing that is not realistic; realism defines itself by its difference from such writing. A similar economy operates in Trollope's novels: poetry and romance are admitted into the lives of Trollope's characters, but only within confines that neutralize their attractions and point out their difference from the real. In Lizzie Eustace's case, the power of poetry is denied by its result; Lizzie's error is the application of a proper mode of reading to an improper book, one that cannot reward the reading that *The Eustace Diamonds* itself invites. For Lady Glencora, poetry and romance are a phase of immaturity, through which she passes safely because poetry cannot rule for long over a mind that is fundamentally realistic. Along with Trollope's other characters who outgrow poetry, Glencora recapitulates in her development the history of English prose fiction, which also grew up from romances to realistic novels. As the *Autobiography* remarks on Glencora's career after *Can You Forgive Her?* "the romance of her life is gone, but there remains a rich reality of which she is fully able to taste the flavour" (158).

Poetry and romance are also admissible into Trollope's realistic world when they are ironically paired with what negates them. The obese and vulgar Mrs. Moulder in *Orley Farm* is "not without a touch of poetry," because she can describe a well-cooked turkey as "like melted diamonds" (24). In the same novel, it is commendable for Sir Peregrine Orme to act with "poetic chivalry," because he is seventy years old and because such behavior is "not the way of the world" (26). The aged Lady Hartletop in *Phineas Redux* does not "look like a romantic woman; but, in spite of appearances, romance and a duck-like waddle may go together" (25). No character in Trollope's novels, however, indulges in romance without being immature or ludicrous—or evil. Striplings and waddling matrons can be romantic without harm because youth or obesity makes their romance ineffectual in the real world. When a taste for poetry is found in a potent adult, the combination makes for villainy. Lizzie Eustace's silly evil is inseparable from her fondness for Byron, and Trollope's male villains are always characterized as in some way romantic or poetical. Outright villainy is as foreign to Trollope's realistic world as is the heroism that I shall shortly discuss. Trollope's most villainous men are those who act most like stage villains; their behavior is that of a literary stereotype, jarring with the realistic behavior of those who share their fictional world. And such villains are often fond of poetry—like Ferdinand Lopez in *The Prime Minister* or George Vavasor in *Can You Forgive Her?* who by his own declaration is "made up of poetry" (5).

There is in Trollope's fiction a tendency that was to become definitive of late-nineteenth-century naturalism—the tendency to consider as properly "real" only what had not been made literary by other writers, to concentrate on subjects that had been thought too ordinary or unglamorous for literature. Trollope never goes so far as to equate the real with the emetic, as Zola was accused of doing by a later generation of English critics. But literary stereotypes are excluded from his world as unreal, and any Trollope character who believes that poetry and romance exist in the real world is either suspect or misguided. As Trollope wrote to George Eliot in 1863: "You know that my novels are not sensational. In *Rachel Ray* I have attempted to confine myself absolutely to the commonest details of commonplace life among the most ordinary people, allowing myself no incident that would be even remarkable in every day life. I have shorn my fiction of all romance."[9]

Romance is in writing, not in reality. The realistic novelist does not reach out toward reality as a model, but cuts writing back, restraining it within the limits that guarantee equivalence with the real. This, according to Trollope, is the traditional achievement of the English novel, which has always fostered a view of life that is "realistic, practical, and, though upon the whole serviceable, upon the whole also unpoetical rather than romantic."[10] It is a curious tradition, however, because it is bound together only by its continuous equivalence to the real, an equivalence that precludes the influence of one text upon another. Trollope proudly joins his novels to the English tradition, but he never mentions having learned or copied from it.

In the one case where a Trollope novel might seem to be more directly inspired by Thackeray than by life, the *Autobiography* is pointed in its denial: "I believe that Lizzie would have been just as she is though Becky Sharpe had never been described" (296). It is a peculiar feature of Trollope's treatment of Thackeray—whom he admires enough to make

---

[9]Letter to George Eliot, 18 October 1863, *Letters*, p. 138.
[10]"On English Prose Fiction As a Rational Amusement," in *Four Lectures*, ed. Morris L. Parrish (London: Constable, 1938), p. 112.

"influence" a serious question[11] — that at every opportunity he misspells the names of Thackeray's two most famous characters, Becky Sharp(e) and Colonel Newcom(b)e.[12] Freedom from literary influence, however, assures originality of conception, not of language. The language of Trollope's fiction is as unoriginal as possible, making great use of the proverbs, truisms, and clichés that are Glencora's "downright honest figures." These figures are so timeworn that the name of their inventor, if they had one, is no longer attached to them. But Trollope's theory requires, and his novels assert, the complete newness of the only thing in fiction that is not language — character. This newness is not extravagance, nor even invention; sympathy is aided by the ordinariness, and therefore the recognizability, of character. But Trollope's characters are new to writing: they are original to the extent that they have never been written down before.

In Trollope's theory, poetry and romance designate territories outside the boundaries of the realistic novel. They are an airy realm into which writers may soar and readers may be carried, far away from the solid earth of real life. In Trollope's fiction, poetry and romance also name places, and these places, too, are remote from where real life is carried on. As in Lady Glencora's case, romantic scenes may be visited safely by one who knows where they belong. But for an ignoramus like Lizzie Eustace, the shore near Portray Castle is as befuddling as the poetry she reads there. The canny Mrs. Greenow in *Can You Forgive Her?* is even more immune to romance than Lady Glencora. She can marry the romantic Captain Bellfield because romance is neutralized by her commonplace mind and his seedy appearance. She can also identify him with romantic scenery, because the identification is ludicrous. As she tells Kate Vavasor: "I do like a little romance about them — just a sniff, as I call it, of the rocks and valleys. One knows that it doesn't mean much; but it's like artificial flowers, — it gives a little colour, and takes off the dowdiness. Of course, bread-and-cheese is the real thing. The rocks and valleys are no good at all, if you haven't got that." In response to the Captain's most florid declaration of love, Mrs. Greenow replies, "'That's all fudge,'" and the narrator comments, "She would have said, 'all rocks and valleys,' only he would not have understood her." So perfectly does the unwitting Captain

---

[11]For Henry James, there was no question. In his "Anthony Trollope: A Partial Portrait," he bluntly states: "It is probably not unfair to say that if Trollope derived half his inspiration from life, he derived the other half from Thackeray" (reprinted in *Trollope: The Critical Heritage*, ed. Donald Smalley [London: Routledge & Kegan Paul, 1969], p. 537).

[12]Another case is the misspelling of Cinq(ue)bars in chapter 16 of *Can You Forgive Her?*

suit the conditions of this neutralized romance that he can, poetically, be named by the scenery that shares his irrelevance. "That's what aunt Greenow calls a sniff of the rocks and valleys," remarks Alice Vavasor to her cousin Kate, as they observe him tossing a cigar butt into the shrubbery (64).

Rocks and valleys, along with moonlit ruins and rocky seashores, are associated with poetry and romance in several ways. They have so long been the scenes of nonrealistic writing that they are inseparable from it; one cannot envision them free of literature. They are also located on the fringes of the real world, far from the drawing rooms and streets where real life is carried on. They are just that distant, barren zone to which Trollope and his contemporaries would banish the poetic eagle. And they have, like nonrealistic writing, a power of attraction, which is described in both the theory and the novels as an unwholesome pull outward, upward, and away. Not only are poetry and romance interchangeable terms for Trollope, but poetry in his novels is almost always Romantic poetry. The Trollopian notion of poetry and romance is derived from the literature of the late eighteenth and early nineteenth centuries. Everything about the poems and romances of that time is excluded from the Trollopian world, and the exclusion is aided by the slightly archaic quality of such things when they appear in a setting that is otherwise emphatically contemporary. Of all mid-Victorian novelists, only Trollope habitually set his novels in the present day, and the past that they exclude is a literary past as well as a historical one.

Trollope's theory locates the chief value of a novel in its portrayal of character, with the consequent arousal of sympathy in the reader. His novels, similarly, are almost wholly concerned with relations between people. The contemplation of what is greater or merely other than human has no place in either the theory or the fiction. The danger of romantic scenery, like that of Romantic poetry, is its power to lure the mind out of its familiar sphere into regions of majestic obscurity. For Trollope, as for the Gothic imagination of the previous century, nature and art are at their grandest when one cannot quite make them out: "In looking at the grandest works of nature, and of art too, I fancy, it is never well to see all. There should be something left to the imagination, and much should be half-concealed in mystery. The greatest charm of a mountain range is the wild feeling that there must be strange unknown desolate worlds in those far-off valleys beyond."[13] It is appropriate that the villainous, poetical

[13] Trollope was inspired to these reflections by the domesticated sublimity of Niagara Falls, as reported in *North America*, ed. Donald Smalley and Bradford A. Booth (1862; New York: Knopf, 1951), p. 99.

George Vavasor should echo these sentiments: "The poetry and mystery of the mountains are lost to those who make themselves familiar with their details, not the less because such familiarity may have useful results. In this world things are beautiful only because they are not quite seen, or not perfectly understood. Poetry is precious chiefly because it suggests more than it declares" (*Can You Forgive Her?*, 5). Mrs. Radcliffe provides similar scenes and responses in *The Mysteries of Udolpho*; the major difference is that Radcliffe admires the "finer spirit" with which the mind is inspired by "stupendous scenes,"[14] while Trollope sees there only desolation, and the mendacity of a vicious man.

Descriptions of nature are usually perfunctory in Trollope's novels; only human habitations are minutely and carefully described. Even these, however (such as Trollope's admired scenes of country houses), often serve as introductory set pieces—inventories of details provided early in the novels and taken for granted thereafter. Indeed, though Trollope's theory speaks of character as portrait, the physical appearance of characters is often slighted in his novels. Like the description of scenery, the description of faces and bodies is often treated as an irksome but necessary preliminary, which must be gotten out of the way before the real business of the novel can be attended to. The opening chapters of *Doctor Thorne* are an early example of this frequent Trollopian practice. However good the novel's borrowed plot may be, its first two chapters are so static, so clogged with description, that they require an apology:

> I quite feel that an apology is due for beginning a novel with two long dull chapters full of description. I am perfectly aware of the danger of such a course. In so doing I sin against the golden rule which requires us all to put our best foot foremost, the wisdom of which is fully recognized by novelists, myself among the number. . . . This is unartistic on my part, and shows want of imagination as well as want of skill. (2)

The description of Mary Thorne provides occasion for a similar apology: "Of her personal appearance, it certainly is my business as an author to say something. She is my heroine, and, as such, must necessarily be very beautiful; but, in truth, her mind and inner qualities are more clearly distinct to my brain than her outward form and features" (3).

Trollope's attractive young women are often introduced in such a grudging way, as, for example, the Dale sisters in *The Small House at Allington*:

> I am well aware that I have not as yet given any description of Bell and

---

[14]Ann Radcliffe, *The Mysteries of Udolpho*, ed. Bonamy Dobrée (London: Oxford University Press, 1970), pp. 42-43.

Lilian Dale, and equally well aware that the longer the doing so is postponed the greater the difficulty becomes. I wish it could be understood without any description. . . . They were fair-haired girls, very like each other, of whom I have before my mind's eye a distinct portrait, which I fear I shall not be able to draw in any such manner as will make it distinct to others. (6)

One aim of these characteristically Trollopian passages is to distinguish the charm of Trollope's young ladies from mere superficial beauty. You might pass Eleanor Harding in the street, for example, "without notice"; but you could not pass an evening with her "and not lose your heart" (*The Warden*, 11). Another aim, however, is to mark those points where writing is inadequate, where the conventions of literary portrayal fail to provide a satisfactory vehicle for the conveyance of character.

This practice, indulged in at other typical points as well, was a major cause of the denigration that Trollope's novels suffered at the hands of Henry James and other late-Victorian critics. The intrusive author was a common feature of mid-Victorian novels, and Thackeray certainly used the device as extensively as Trollope did; but James's "Partial Portrait" describes this "pernicious trick" as a particularly Trollopian sin, one that James regards with exasperation—and, one might also say, with bewilderment: "He took a suicidal satisfaction in reminding the reader that the story he was telling was only, after all, a make-believe. He habitually referred to the work in hand (in the course of that work) as a novel, and to himself as a novelist, and was fond of letting the reader know that this novelist could direct the course of events according to his pleasure."[15] There is a curious misunderstanding in the last sentence. As Wayne Booth has pointed out, it is the telling of the events, not the events themselves, that is called into question by such "intrusions."[16]

James goes on to a further misunderstanding, however, which Booth does not correct. The effect of such passages, according to James, is to remind the reader that the novel is "an arbitrary thing";[17] and Booth agrees that, though "the characters' lives are inviolable," the "relation of the author and reader to those lives" is subject to manipulation.[18] According to Trollope's theory, however, neither life nor writing is supposed to be arbitrary. The characters live independently of the novels written about them, and every word of those novels is precise and unchangeable. The proper effect of such passages—evidently not their actual effect, but the one that Trollope's theory would require—is indeed to inform the

---

[15]James, *Critical Heritage*, p. 535.
[16]*The Rhetoric of Fiction* (Chicago: University of Chicago Press, 1961), p. 206.
[17]James, *Critical Heritage*, p. 536.
[18]*Rhetoric of Fiction*, p. 206.

reader that the story could have been told otherwise, but only if the medium of writing were better than it ever can be. If the story were told differently, the novel would be inferior; only a better medium (which is impossible) would produce a better novel.

The mechanism is a typical one: it is the favorite compensatory maneuver of the novel-machine. Writing is given to the novelist; he must do the best he can with what is available. When the Trollopian narrator "intrudes" upon his story, he does so because the conventions of story-telling have interefered with the story to be told. Among these conventions is the rule that a novel must have only three volumes; the narrator of *Barchester Towers*, in a passage that Booth quotes, cries out, "Oh, that Mr. Longman would allow me a fourth!" (43). Another convention is that scenes and heroines must be described and must be beautiful; I have cited some examples of how the Trollopian novel meets this requirement. James correctly gauged the "deliberately inartistic" quality of such intrusions. They are just as inartistic as the Trollopian novelist himself, who struggles to make a recalcitrant medium convey what is other and better than itself. The text of a novel has no value in Trollope's theory, and the intrusions that most offended James denigrate only the text, not what is to be seen through it. Indeed, Trollope's theory requires that the novelist lay aside his "identity" when he writes, so that the narrator who puts down his narration is only a function of the text. The text puts itself down, encouraging the reader to look beyond the text at what is real. It is a typical tactic of Trollope's fiction that when it obeys literary conventions, it does so blatantly, grudgingly. Literature is different from and only partially adequate to life, and literature itself announces its inferiority.

The beginnings and endings of Trollope's novels are common occasions for self-advertised inadequacy. The apologetic opening of *Doctor Thorne* is a notable example, but the tactic is repeated frequently throughout Trollope's career. The first four chapters of *The Eustace Diamonds* are a makeshift substitute for a *dramatis personae:* "the poor narrator has been driven to expend his four first chapters in the mere task of introducing his characters. He regrets the length of these introductions, and will now begin at once the action of his story" (4). *Is He Popenjoy?* begins with two "Introductory" chapters, awkwardly labeled "Number One" and "Number Two." This is also a makeshift strategy. The novelist would prefer "that it were possible so to tell a story that a reader should beforehand know every detail of it up to a certain point, or be so circumstanced that he might be supposed to know." This is the case in "telling the little novelettes of our life," but unfortunately "such stories as those I have to tell cannot be written after that fashion" (1).

Endings are just as conventional as beginnings, and even more frequently announced to be so. One of James's citations is the first sentence of the last chapter of *Barsetshire Towers:* "The end of a novel, like the end of a children's dinner party, must be made up of sweetmeats and sugarplums" (53). This is, as James calls it, an early instance of a later habit. The last chapter of *Framley Parsonage* is entitled "How They Were All Married, Had Two Children, and Lived Happily Ever After." *Ayala's Angel* introduces its last chapter with a bit of arch self-congratulation:

> Now we have come to our last chapter, and it may be doubted whether any reader,—unless he be some one specially gifted with a genius for statistics, —will have perceived how very many people have been made happy by matrimony. If marriage be the proper ending for a novel,—the only ending as this writer takes it to be, which is not discordant,—surely no tale was ever so properly ended, or with so full a concord, as this one. (64)

Sometimes the obedience of convention turns ironic or even nasty, like the last paragraph of *He Knew He Was Right*, which announces that, though Giles Hickbody and Martha are "not actually married as yet" —both are servants, and both over sixty—"it is quite understood that the young people are engaged, and are to be made happy together at some future time" (99). And the final chapter of *Doctor Wortle's School* opens with this dour reminder of *Framley Parsonage:*

> I cannot pretend that the reader shall know, as he ought to be made to know, the future fate and fortunes of our personages. They must be left still struggling. But then is not such always in truth the case, even when the happy marriage has been celebrated—even when, in the course of two rapid years, two normal children make their appearance to gladden the hearts of their parents? (24)

The same effect can be created by declaring a convention served as by proclaiming it violated. In either case, the convention is set aside as a literary matter, having nothing to do with life. The Trollopian novel treats literary conventions as it does all such purely written things, bowing to them as to requirements imposed from without and against the author's will, but at the same time incorporating them into its own rhetoric of reality.

Trollope's theory defines character as living and continuous, so that to make any beginning or ending at all in its narration is to observe a rule foreign to the truth of what is portrayed. The reader's supposed expectation that novels will begin and end in certain ways is taught to him only by literature. No amount of living-with can teach a novelist how to begin and end his books; only other books can teach him that. Like poetry and romance, beginnings and endings are alien to the Trollopian world of transparent texts and real people. But first and last words cannot simply be excluded; they are unavoidable signs that the realistic novel is just as much a written text as any poem or romance. Trollope's rhetoric handles this necessity in a characteristic fashion: declaring the observance or defiance of literary conventions, it degrades its textuality while asserting the nontextual reality that the written text can only imperfectly convey. The treatment has a characteristic double effect. On the one hand, it devalues the novel's text and its author, portraying the one as awkward and the other as almost incompetent. On the other hand, however, the treatment draws attention to the thing it devalues, making Trollope's novels far more self-referential than his theory would seem to allow. That this self-referentiality is usually either cute, clumsy, or cranky only limits its effect. When the Trollopian text speaks for itself in the person of its narrator, it asserts its own literary nature; but it does so negatively, achieving thereby the simultaneous assertion and denial that is typical of the novel-machine in all its operations.

Poetry and romance are conventional ways of writing, and all written things must begin and end. Even in character, however—that part of a Trollopian novel that is not supposed to be written—there are literary conventions that the reader may be expected to know from his experience of books. It is a book-learned rule that a novel must have a heroine or a hero. Commenting on Hawthorne's metaphor of a world under glass, the *Autobiography* declares that it has always been Trollope's aim to let his readers "recognise human beings like to themselves"—that is, without "exaggerated baseness" or "excellence" (125). The chief merit of *Framley Parsonage* is that it offers "no heroism and no villainy" (123), and there is a realistic reason for their absence:

> The young man who in a novel becomes a hero . . . by trickery, falsehood, and flash cleverness, will have many followers, whose attempt to rise in the world ought to lie heavily on the conscience of the novelists who create fictitious Cagliostros. There are Jack Sheppards other than those who break into houses and out of prisons,—Macheaths, who deserve the gallows worse than Gay's hero. (189)

Those who imitate any fiction but Trollope's are doomed to real trouble: reality contains villains whom no writing but the realistic kind is competent to portray. It takes only common sense to understand that pure heroism and pure villainy are rare in the world, though both are common in books. But the common sense that governs Trollope's mixed characters, his vacillating heroes and partly sympathetic villains, is as much a literary stance as a sensitive reflection of reality. Heroes, heroines, and villains may be impossible creatures, but literature has known many of them. Their exclusion from the Trollopian novel is another declaration that that novel is reality itself, not literature.

Trollope's novels seldom use the word "villain." His evil characters do not spin plots; their evil is usually constitutional in its source and haphazard in its enactment. Trollope's closest approach to a plot-spinning villain is Mr. Scarborough in *Mr. Scarborough's Family*, who has "prepared a romance" for the beguilement of his heirs (1) and who "had begun scheming early in the business" (54), like a sensation novelist who plots his fictions in advance. But even Mr. Scarborough's sensationalism has something Trollopian about it, since "he had not made up his mind" to use his Collinsesque plot "till but a short time before he had put it in practice" (2). Considerable sympathy is elicited for the helpless and dying man, whose body is "one mass of cuts and bruises" (7). His is a complex case of what Ruth apRoberts has called Trollope's casuistry, his habit of finding something in even the darkest character to argue for.[19]

The technique is widespread in the novels, often depending on such phrases as "giving due" or "doing justice." In *Framley Parsonage*, for example, justice is done in turn to Emily Dunstable (24), Mr. Sowerby (27), Griselda Grantly (29), and the archdeacon (40), always at a point where the reader's judgment is said to be turning against them. In *The Small House at Allington*, Adolphis Crosbie's due can be given him even in the most extreme case: "But Crosbie was not a man to commit suicide. In giving him his due I must protest that he was too good for that. He knew too well that a pistol-bullet could not be the be-all and the end-all here, and there was too much manliness in him for so cowardly an escape" (28). In *The Prime Minister*, Lopez is an "evil genius" (47), a "dreadful incubus" (58), and "all a lie from head to foot" (73), but even so he gets justice done him: "To give him his due, he did not know that he was a villain" (54). Lady Carbury in *The Way We Live Now* is at least as false as Lopez, but so much justice is done her that the falseness is almost canceled out: "The woman was false from head to foot, but there was much good in her false though she was" (2). And even Fred Neville in *An Eye for an Eye*, who seduces and abandons Kate O'Hara, "was not a villain—simply a self-indulgent spoiled young man who had realised to himself no idea of duty in life" (12).

[19] *Trollope: Artist and Moralist* (London: Chatto & Windus, 1971), p. 53.

The list of examples could be extended: "giving due" is one of Trollope's commonest strategies. Its ubiquity reveals a subtle conception of human nature, but giving due is also consistent with the rhetoric of containment and limitation found everywhere in Trollope's theory and practice. The writer's chief temptation is that writing will make him exaggerate; character itself is limitation, and Trollope's justified villains are limited as well as humanized by their justification. A similar strategy is employed in Trollope's treatment of his heroes and heroines, who always have some flaw or weakness that leads them into difficulties. Here, however, the case is made even more explicitly. The terms "hero" and "heroine" are conventional, like the conventional marriages in a novel's last chapter, and they are handled with even greater irony. Both are literary categories; realistic novels do not contain them, and Trollope becomes a novelist when he ceases to be the "hero" of his youthful dreams. The reader who comes to a Trollope novel with these categories impressed on his mind by other books is often told that the categories will be rearranged or left empty. The hero of *The Small House at Allington*, for example, is "cut up, as it were, into fragments": "Whatever of the magnificent may be produced will be diluted and apportioned out in very moderate quantities among two or more, probably among three or four, young gentlemen—to none of whom will be vouchsafed the privilege of much heroic action" (2). Neither Lizzie Eustace nor Lucy Morris is the "real heroine" of *The Eustace Diamonds:*

> The real heroine, if it be found possible to arrange her drapery becomingly, and to put that part which she enacted into properly heroic words, shall stalk in among us at some considerably later period of the narrative, when the writer shall have accustomed himself to the flow of words, and have worked himself up to a state of mind fit for the reception of noble acting and noble speaking. (3)

No such being, of course, ever arrives. The realistic writer never gets accustomed enough to the flow of his words to produce such a thoroughly literary monstrosity.

Sometimes heroism is linked to the kinds of excluded literature that are its proper province, thereby excluding heroism along with its scene. The Marquis of Brotherton in *Is He Popenjoy?* is fittingly called "the hero of these mysteries" (51), and Colonel Osborne in *He Knew He Was Right*, reflecting on the unlikelihood of his running away with another man's wife, is "aware that he was no longer fit to be the hero of such a romance as that" (20). In both these cases, heroism is neutralized still more effectively by its attachment to distinctly unheroic characters—the one a syphilitic libertine, the other an aging roué whose chief concern is to study "the wrinkles beneath his eyes, so that in conversation they might be as little apparent as possible" (20). It is probably true that there is as little heroism in real life as there is villainy, but in Trollope's novels fidelity to life is often the same as the rejection of fiction—all fiction, that is, but Trollope's own.

As in the case of poetry and romance, the categories of villainy and heroism are a bit antiquated. Except for the sensation novel, which was something of a throwback in this and other respects, the novels of Trollope's contemporaries were fully sensitive to the mixed quality of human character, as they were to the unpoetical, unromantic nature of everyday life. Trollope's characters seldom mention novels, but when they do they usually agree with Isabella Dale that novels are untrue to life: "But if we are to have real life," she tells her sister, "let it be real" (*The Small House at Allington*, 42). The attitude is exactly that which the *Autobiography* condemns, the idea that a taste for novels is "vain if not vicious" (187). Or it is the attitude of Signora Neroni in *Barchester Towers*, who announces to the oozily amorous Mr. Slope, "There is no happiness in love, except at the end of an English novel" (27). But these are not Trollope's own novels, nor can they be the novels of Trollope's great contemporaries in realism. They sound more like the novels of Mrs. Radcliffe and the Minerva Press, novels of the same period as the poetry and romances that color Trollope's employment of those terms. Trollope never acknowledges, in theory or in practice, that any fiction rivals his own in its mastery of real life. The conventions that he simultaneously accepts and rejects are an inheritance; they are the conventions of his parents' day much more than of his own.

Yet the effect of such treatment is to call into question any literary inheritance, just because it is literary, and to assert the primacy of the one kind of novel with nothing willingly literary about it—the Trollopian kind. The ultimate definition of Trollopian realism is that its products are not fiction at all but pieces of real life, and the rhetoric of both the theory and the practice consistently devalues any fiction that does not attempt to suppress its unavoidable difference from the real. Trollope's sharpest criticisms are made against those kinds of writing, chiefly poetry and sensational romances, that not only fail to suppress their difference but that also accentuate it. In this, Trollope goes from general agreement with his contemporaries to a private extreme far beyond them. Many critics of the sensation novel condemned it for untruthfulness to life, but many more found it untrue to art as well, because it falsified life in the wrong way. Bigamy and murder did occur in the world, and a fictional treatment of them was therefore "realistic" to some degree. But in one reviewer's commonplace opinion, it was the novelist's duty not to reproduce the "apparently disconnected and broken threads" of modern life, but "to connect its broken parts and pieces, and to explain away its discrepancies, presenting it to us as an ideal whole, a Cosmos."[20] In perhaps an inadvertently perceptive way, Trollope's contemporaries often criticized him for having failed at this duty, merely "photographing" the real instead of molding it into artistic shape. Such critics were missing the complex (and certainly artistic) structure of Trollope's fiction, but they were correctly responding to its rhetoric, and his theory commends their mistake. Trollope's novels are far from inartistic, but they pretend to be anything but art. They pretend to be the only kind of writing that can give back life as it really is, because they are life itself.

No reader (except possibly Trollope himself) is capable of the total surrender to the reality of Trollope's fiction that his theory desires and his practice encourages. Indeed, if such a surrender were possible, it would spoil the novel's role as a teacher. Only when the *Autobiography* deals with the novel's teaching does it admit that the novelist alters reality in making an equivalent of it. He does nothing to the real, but he does make a selection from its features, and he rearranges them to make "virtue alluring and vice ugly, while he charms his reader instead of wearying him" (190). A good deal of the advice that the *Autobiography* gives to aspiring novelists has to do with arrangement; I will discuss this part of the theory in chapter 7. But the theory avoids drawing the plain conclusion that any alteration of reality, even if it is only rearrangement, enforces the difference between fiction and life and clouds the glass that separates the reader's from the characters' world. Teaching depends on sympathy, but sympathy comes from equivalence, and equivalence is compromised by teaching.

The whole matter of teaching is an incongruous part of Trollope's theory, since the justification of the spectacular mechanism of the novel-machine seems to be little more than that its products show young ladies and gentlemen how to go about courting each other. This is not its justification for the novelist, whose real life is founded on fiction and fed by it. But the reader is incurably different from the novelist, because in the reader's case fiction is supported by real life, not the reverse. For the reader, fiction must be supplemented by writing and publication; it must also be justified, or at least excused, by teaching. Yet the greatest effort of

[20] "Miss Braddon, The Illuminated Newgate Calendar," *Eclectic and Congregational Review* 14 (January 1868): 23.

Trollope's rhetoric, in both theory and practice, is aimed at an effect that, if it were achieved, would efface writing, wipe out the marks of publication, and preclude teaching—because a reader whose life is fully real can hardly learn much from seeing more of what he already knows. No reader requires fiction as the Trollopian novelist does. For readers, fiction is a supplement, a recreation, or a lesson; it is not the foundation of life, as it is for the novelist. The *Autobiography* provides clear justification for Trollope's desire to make fiction absolutely equivalent to life, but it fails to explain why this most important of activities should be of any value to a reader, who is already immersed in life and who might desire literature specifically for its difference.

Writing Love

I HAVE SHOWN in the preceding chapter how one aspect of Trollope's theory—the distinction of realistic writing from all other kinds—is duplicated in the novels as a polemic against nonrealistic fiction and in favor of the Trollopian kind, which is competent to all of life, including other fiction. This discussion led to the introduction of a new problem: the degree to which Trollope's writings are neither typically realistic nor typically mid-Victorian but distinctively and personally Trollopian. One might want to say at this point that Trollope's theory and practice are equal emanations from the man who devised them both and that therefore they can be traced back equally to him, their common source. But it would be a precisely Trollopian reading of Trollope that would take his writing to be a window on an unwritten, living human being. There is no qualitative difference between reading the *Autobiography* as a story about a real man and reading Trollope's novels as stories about real people. Both readings would be recommended by Trollope's theory; the only practical difference would be that we know from other documents that Anthony Trollope was once alive, while the absence of such documents informs us that his characters never were. The difference is great enough, of course, but the reading is the same; and to read in a Trollopian way is to obey Trollope's rhetoric, not to criticize it.

My endeavor has been to read Trollope in an anti-Trollopian way, seeing his texts in relation to each other and not to the reality that those

texts convey. It may seem that this has led to nothing more than turning
Trollope upside down—putting first whatever he puts last, and wherever
he writes "reality" replacing it with "writing." Yet it has been possible, I
think, to show that the world that the *Autobiography* describes, a world
made of nothing but writing, is the foundation of the world that the
Autobiography says is there, a world of anything but writing. The
ingenious economy of the novel-machine is set in motion by the imposition of the real on the written. Unwritten reality must be writable, even
though reality is known by its difference from writing and writing is by
nature inadequate to reality. There is no synthesis of these antitheses;
they are in perpetual disequilibrium, and Trollope's rhetoric aims only at
making them work, not sublimating them. This imbalance is characteristic
of literary realism—or indeed of any writing that attempts to convey the
real world. But it is also a particularly Trollopian phenomenon, marking
all his writing just as distinctively as that other mark, his name, which
says that this writing came from this man and no other. The most
distinctive feature of Trollope's theory is the thoroughness with which it
pits writing against writing.

In chapter 5, my anti-Trollopian reading of Trollope outlined how
the fiction, which is explicitly about life and nothing else, is also about
literature and the place of that fiction in it. Trollope's characters define
the scene and structure of their lives by the exclusion from the real world
of certain places and courses of action. But these places and courses are
also literary categories, which Trollope's novels exclude as his theory
does, by declaring them to be unreal. The economy of both theory and
practice is the same: the excluded thing is also included, neutralized by its
opposite, and the real world, like realistic writing, is defined by its
difference from what it is not. By placing themselves in relation to other
kinds of fiction, Trollope's novels do acknowledge that they, too, are
texts like the others. But the relation is negative. Trollope's novels are
nontexts, antitexts: they are about themselves only to the degree that
they advertise their inadequacy to the reality that they nevertheless
completely convey. Other texts are artful and artificial; Trollope's are
honest.

Trollope's novels are also antiliterary, insofar as they deny their
more than accidental kinship to other novels. Trollope's novels are turned
fully away from themselves, toward the real world. Nothing they convey
has been learned from writing; it has all come from life. Again, an intertextual relation is implied even in the denial of one, and Trollope's novels
make full use of the literary conventions that they mock and criticize.

Yet, by a typical rhetorical maneuver, these conventions are set aside as unfortunately necessary but irrelevant to the truth of the matter, life. Such conventions join plot among the baggage that the business of novel making has forced upon a novelist who would rather have things otherwise but who diligently makes do. This is a rhetorical strategy, sustained by a literary practice as sophisticated as anyone's has ever been. But the sophistication disguises itself everywhere, in theory and practice alike, in the convincing form of naïveté, apology, and incompetence. A greater prize is to be attained than praise for one's literary cleverness. Severing themselves from tradition, convention, and even skill, Trollope's novels lay claim to what no more artful artist would dare to assert—complete mastery over life. By their own declaration, Trollope's novels are the greatest, the ultimate novels. They have disentangled themselves from the romance of writing and stand forth triumphantly transparent, life itself.

There is a kind of tyranny, as I suggested in the last chapter, in the definition of "life" that Trollope's novels preach while pretending to report it. "Life" is restricted to interpersonal relations, and to those within a fairly limited range. Ecstasy is excluded, as are the encounters with Nature and God of which the Romantic poets wrote. Higher flights of the imagination (even the metaphor damns itself) have no place in the Trollopian world, and therefore no place in life. Nowhere in Trollope's fiction is there a study of a mind devoted to the exploration of an ideal or even a concept; there is nothing comparable to George Eliot's Dorothea, Lydgate, or Daniel Deronda. Trollope's closest approach to such a character is Mr. Crawley in the Barsetshire novels, but even he is dealt with chiefly as an uncomfortable person to have at table, and at the end of *The Last Chronicle of Barset* he is "conquered"—dressed in new, acceptable clothes, awkwardly discussing foxes with the Archdeacon (83).

I do not mean to suggest that Trollope was incapable of conceptual thinking or that he was merely a characteristic British Philistine. It may be that the limits within which Trollope encloses life do contain most of it, that artists, poets, and men devoted to ideas are in truth the peripheral creatures his fiction makes them out to be. But, true or not, Trollope's definition of life is made by his fiction as much as observed by it, and that definition is a very limited one. Its locus is the drawing room—those "coarse, inappropriate surroundings" from which Lizzie Eustace flees with Shelley—and its overriding concern is the interaction of people in such a setting. These limitations are already present in the scene of living-with, where Trollope conceives his novels. There is nothing in that scene but people, and no goal is in view from that portable, invisible drawing room but the achievement of sympathy. The reader, too, will have no other goal, and in the world of Trollope's characters nothing else is of real value. Trollope while he conceives, the reader while he reads, and the characters while they live are all engaged in the same project, and all of them, theoretically or fictionally, go about it in the same way.

Trollope's theory of conception and reading is, in its peculiar way, an epistemology, a theory of knowing. It has nothing to say about existence. "Reality" is not the same as existence; the theory deals with a great many things that, though they undoubtedly exist, are not "real." Reality is a sense of recognition and an attribution of value; both reader and character are equally real, though the one exists and the other does not. The theory also has little to say about the origins and ends of knowledge. Origins, as I have shown, are problematical in the *Autobiography*. In the novels, though many of Trollope's characters might be said to mature, their characteristics are already established, often stubbornly so, when the novels begin. Trollope never wrote a Bildungsroman, unless it is the *Autobiography*. His theory and practice are both concerned with knowing as a process carried on among fully developed intelligences whose origins and destinies are inquired into as little as their existence is. Knowledge is, in this sense, its own end: the best thing a realistic novel can do is to bring about a state of complete sympathy between reader and character, and the best thing that can happen to a Trollope character is to achieve that state with another one. This is the highest value; this is real.

Trollope's novels, because they describe the workings of the mind, might be called psychological. But though they are very much concerned with mental processes, they give no attention to the structure of the mind as such. Nor do they recognize any fundamental difference between internal thought processes and external events. The world is structured just as the mind is, and perfect adjustment is possible between the two. Like George Eliot, Trollope is interested above all in the difficulties that beset the mind in its relation to the external world, chiefly composed of other minds. But in George Eliot's novels, the mind is irremediably different from the world about it. Its laws are not the same, and even between two sympathetic minds there may be such a difference of internal language that understanding is possible only by means of necessarily approximate translation. Freudian psychoanalysis also depends on such a difference. For Freud, neurosis is distinguished from health by the practical question of whether the patient's everyday activities are impeded by his psychical processes. Psychoanalysis can remove whatever impediments are susceptible of removal, but the state of being alive is one of permanent maladjustment; complete equilibrium between the mind and its environment is death. Trollope recognizes the complexities of minds in interaction, but in his novels all differences are accidental. They can be overcome by effort, and in very few cases among Trollope's characters does the effort wholly fail. For Trollope, the world and all the minds in it speak the same language. Characters are capable, as novelist and reader ought to be capable, of complete and accurate sympathy. And the difficulties that the characters face in Trollope's novels are the same as those that his theory attempts to minimize in the writing and reading of novels.

Though Trollope's novels do not describe the mind as such, they assume that it has a particular structure. The Trollopian mind contains two faculties, which occasionally bear the misleading labels "conscious" and "unconscious." Both of these faculties are voices. The conscious voice is articulate, fluent, and superficial; the unconscious voice speaks for those things that lie, almost literally, closest to the character's heart. The Trollopian unconscious, however, should not be mistaken for the Freudian concept that goes by the same name. It was one of Freud's major redefinitions of the term that unconscious processes need not ever become conscious, that almost all "thoughts" originate in the unconscious but only some of them are capable of entering consciousness. Trollope's use of the term more closely resembles the pre-Freudian concept of "unconscious cerebration"—a process not different in kind from conscious thinking, running parallel to it, and conducted in the same language, without necessity of symbolic translation. Trollope's characters, indeed, are about equally aware of both their conscious and their unconscious thoughts. In regard to both they possess a third faculty that listens, and that acts upon the advice given to it by either the conscious or the unconscious voice. Both voices are rhetorical, oratorical: the Trollopian mind is a sort of internal debating society, containing an audience and two speakers who compete for their listener's attention. The difference between the orators is principally one of value: the unconscious voice is always the right one, and those of Trollope's characters who achieve happiness do so because, after however long a period of vacillation, they allow the unconscious voice to tell them what to do.

The conscious faculty of the Trollopian mind works by argument, telling, and teaching. Such logical tactics always meet resistance—as in the case of Lord Lufton, who goes to Chaldicotes "not satisfied with himself indeed, but repeating to himself a great many arguments why he should be so satisfied" (*Framley Parsonage*, 3). The resistance often amounts to the contradiction of what has just been consciously asserted. After the death of the old Duke of Omnium, Madame Goesler asks herself the question, "What was it that she wanted?" The answer is double, though unambiguous: "She was ashamed to tell herself that it was love. But she knew this,—that it was necessary for her happiness that she should devote herself to some one" (*Phineas Redux*, 30). Though Trollope's theory seeks to justify the novel by making it a teacher, his characters are never more wrong than when they teach themselves something—like Marie Melmotte, all of whose problems have come about because she "had taught herself this business of falling in love as a lesson, rather than felt it" (*The Way We Live Now*, 98). Self-teaching easily leads to fanaticism, as in the case of Jacob Brattle, who "brooded over injuries done to him,—injuries real or fancied,—till he taught himself to wish that all who hurt him might be crucified for the hurt they did to him" (*The Vicar of Bullhampton*, 5). Or teaching may simply fail altogether, particularly in matters of love: "These lessons, when they have been well learned, have ever come without direct teaching" (*Sir Harry Hotspur of Humblethwaite*, 2).

This collision of teaching with truth is the typical dynamic of the Trollopian mind, extending the full length of some very long novels. A typical passage from *The Small House at Allington* will illustrate the nature of the process:

> In the meantime Lady Alexandrina endeavoured to realise to herself all the advantages and disadvantages of her own position. . . . She had asked herself many times whether her present life was so happy as to make her think that a permanent continuance in it would suffice for her desires, and she had always replied to herself that she would fain change to some other life if it were possible. She had also questioned herself as to her rank, of which she was quite sufficiently proud, and had told herself that she could not degrade herself in the world without a heavy pang. But she had at last taught herself to believe that she had more to gain by becoming the wife of such a man as Crosbie than by remaining as an unmarried daughter of her father's house.

Self-dialogue continues for two more paragraphs, then comes to this typical conclusion: "If she entertained any inner feeling that Crosbie's fault in jilting Lilian Dale was less than it would have been had she herself not been an earl's daughter,—that her own rank did in some degree extenuate her lover's falseness,—she did not express it in words even to herself" (27). The effort of realization passes through stages of question and answer, enforced thought, and teaching, all of which are articulate though not spoken aloud. All of them are also irrelevant, or at least superficial. The determining statement, which is a "feeling" unexpressed in words, comes at the end of the effort and decides the question. Lady Alexandrina is a minor character in *The Small House at Allington*, and her mind is neither sharp nor sensitive; but she thinks in a typical Trollopian way, moving from debate to teaching to feeling, all in the name of self-realization.

Trollopian narrative shifts easily from the description of events in chronological sequence to the analysis of thinking out of time. Events can usually be located in a fictional calendar, while thinking is often analyzed retrospectively, as having occurred sometime between or during events that have already been narrated. The conscious faculty of the Trollopian mind is structured like time—a linear, more or less logical sequence of alternatives, possibilities, and choices. The unconscious faculty, however, which takes precedence over logic, does not assert itself as the consequence of conscious thinking or the end product of it. Unconscious thinking does not depend on reason, and it often makes statements that, as in Lady Alexandrina's case, are unreasonable by comparison with the careful deductive thinking that they follow and terminate. Conscious thinking tells, teaches, and debates; unconscious thinking simply states the truth. It is an odd feature of Trollopian psychology that such truth seldom gets stated without a conscious prologue, sometimes a very long one, but that the truth is found always to have preceded thought and to exist independently of it. There is no necessary link between conscious reasoning and unconscious truth, but the one must be put through its inadequate paces before the leap to the other can be made.

I have called unconscious thinking "truth," but it is that in no absolute way. It is the truth of the thinker's own feelings and desires, stated in a fully accurate form. It is a true statement of character, and, like character itself in Trollope's theory, it is neither imitated from outside nor deduced from prior reasoning. When the truth is arrived at, it is found to have always been there, waiting for words. Sometimes this truth operates without conscious prologue, pushing itself partially into consciousness and dictating behavior without reference to logic. In *The Eustace Diamonds*, Lucy Morris decides to move in with the prickly Lady Linlithgow for a number of practical reasons:

> But Lucy had told the tale to her lover, and her lover approved of her going. Perhaps there was acting upon her mind some feeling, of which she was hardly conscious, that as long as she remained at Fawn Court she would not see her lover. She had told him that she could make herself supremely happy in the simple knowledge that he loved her. But we all know how few such

declarations should be taken as true. Of course she was longing to see him.
. . . She had no formed idea in her own mind that she would be able to see
him should she go to Lady Linlithgow, but still there would be the chances of
her altered life. (33)

Women are better than men at such double thinking, but both sexes
depend on the guidance of feelings that have made themselves known
without articulation:

Women doubt every day, who solve their doubts at last on the right side,
driven to do so, some by fear, more by conscience, but most of them by that
half-prudential, half-unconscious knowledge of what is fitting, useful, and
best under the circumstances, which rarely deserts either men or women till
they have brought themselves to the Burgo Fitzgerald state of recklessness.
(*Can You Forgive Her?*, 50)

Even Burgo Fitzgerald is saved from being a villain because he "seemed to
think so little of himself" (29). He shares this redeeming lack of self-
personality with Felix Carbury, who "never showed consciousness of his
beauty" (*The Way We Live Now*, 2), and with Phineas Finn, who "had
never shown himself to be conscious of his own personal advantages"
(*Phineas Finn*, 6). Even such a treacherous trait as masculine beauty can
be contained, if it is never consciously remarked.

The Trollopian unconscious is the site of truth for men and women,
good and bad alike. Thinking of any conscious kind is both dubious and
unnecessary; one can lead a perfectly successful life without it. "One
forms half the conclusions of one's life," comments the narrator of *Framley
Parsonage*, "without any distinct knowledge that the premises have even
passed through one's mind" (35). Indeed, one is better off if one can get
along without thought: "When he can decide without thinking, then he
can decide without a doubt, and with perfect satisfaction" (*Sir Harry
Hotspur of Humblethwaite*, 20). A career in Parliament almost requires
freedom from thought. Phineas Finn's chief regret after his murder trial is
that now he "could never more enjoy that freedom from self-consciousness, that inner tranquillity of spirit, which are essential to public utility"
(*Phineas Redux*, 67). Conscious thinking is always inferior to unconscious
feeling, even when the latter can make itself only dimly known through a
screen of argumentation. Again, these values have nothing to do with
abstract notions of justice or truth. Feeling is superior to thinking because
it is a clearer medium; it accurately describes the character who feels it.
Character exists prior to all argument, and in some way or other,
consciously or not, character will dictate behavior. As Mr. Whittlestaff
reflects in Trollope's last completed novel:

Mrs. Baggett had understood accurately the nature of his character; but had not understood that, as was his character, so must he act. He could not alter his own self. He could not turn round upon himself, and bid himself be other than he was. It is necessary to be stern and cruel and determined, a man should say to himself. General good will come out of such a line of conduct. But unless he be stern and cruel in other matters also, — unless he has been born stern and cruel, or has so trained himself, — he cannot be stern and cruel for that occasion only. (*An Old Man's Love*, 11)

One is in closest touch with oneself — one is identical with oneself — when one can say, with Mary Lowther in *The Vicar of Bullhampton*, "My own feelings tell me so" (4).

The old-fashioned distinction of thought from feeling, with their separate sources in the head and the heart, probably describes Trollope's map of the mind more appropriately than the distinction of conscious from unconscious, with its post-Trollopian, chiefly Freudian connotations. But Trollope's psychology, primitive and even unpsychological as it may otherwise be, has some modern features. Both thought and feeling are discourses, and both are addressed to a listener who is both the same as and other than the speaker. The value of feeling resides in its equivalence with the listener: otherness disappears, and the discourse *is* the character who feels it. Conscious discourse, "thought," never loses its otherness. Argument, teaching, self-consciousness — all the manifestations of "thought" contain the duality that feeling eradicates. The conscious message is never the same as its recipient; it is always a sort of first draft for character. The unconscious message, like realistic writing, states character immediately, with total and permanent accuracy — a feat that it can accomplish, as realistic writing does, because it is not a report on character, not a sign for it, but character itself.

Trollope claims in the *Autobiography* that "I have never found myself thinking much about the work that I had to do till I was doing it. I have indeed for many years almost abandoned the effort to think, trusting myself . . . to work the matter out when the pen is in my hand" (134). Toward the end of *Phineas Finn*, its hero has arrived at a similar state of practiced thoughtlessness. While waiting to address the House of Commons, Phineas "thought not at all of the words that he was to say": "He had prepared his matter but had prepared no words. He knew that words would come readily enough to him, and that he had learned the task of turning his thoughts quickly into language while standing with a crowd of listeners around him, — as a practised writer does when seated in his chair" (75). Writing and "the art of the orator" are the same (*Autobiography*, 203); both depend on the unpremeditated precision of a discourse that must be true because it is the same as what it says. Living finds its truth in the same equivalence. Living, like novel making, is a rhetorical art.

The distinctive paradox of Trollopian "character" is that, at the same time, it is both writing and the opposite of writing, reality. The whole novel-machine can be thought of as a mechanism for maintaining this paradox. In the novels, the discourse of feeling is marked by the same contradiction: feeling speaks, but what it says is not language. In *The Prime Minister*, Ferdinand Lopez arrives at the truth of his feelings toward Emily Wharton after a paragraph of "thinking" and "musing to himself": "So much he said, palpably, though to himself, with his inner voice. Then,—impalpably, with no even inner voice,—he asked himself what chance he might have of prevailing with the girl herself; and he almost ventured to tell himself that in that direction he need not despair" (2). In *Mr. Scarborough's Family*, Florence Mountjoy's mind has nothing in common with Lopez's but the ability to speak this contradictory language without words:

> Of one thing she was quite certain. Let them . . . think and say what they would of Harry, she would be true to him. . . . She did not say this to herself. By saying it even to herself she would have committed some default of truth. She did not whisper it even to her own heart. But within her heart there was a feeling that, let Harry be right or wrong in what he had done . . . still to her he should be braver, more noble, more manly, more worthy of being loved, than was any other man. (15)

Trollope's characters have the same skill that distinguishes the realistic novelist—the skill of using language to convey its own absence.

The paradox of the unconscious voice is not usually stated so bluntly, but the truth of feeling is always described as resistant to the articulate analyses and deductions that characterize "thinking." As the happy ending of the novel is about to be announced to her, Mary Thorne "could not analyse her own feelings, or give a reason for her own confidence; but she certainly did feel, and even trust, that something was going to happen" (*Doctor Thorne*, 46). For Emily Wharton, beginning to realize the truth about Ferdinand Lopez, feeling rebels violently against thought: "But she could not bring herself to say that Arthur Fletcher had behaved badly. She could not lie. She knew well that his conduct had been noble and generous. Then unconsciously and involuntarily,—or rather in opposition to her own will and inward efforts,—her mind would draw comparisons between her husband and Arthur Fletcher" (*The Prime Minister*, 31). But it is only occasionally so difficult in Trollope's novels to speak by other means than language. In fact, except in cases of drastic disagreement between feelings and reasonable arguments, Trollope's characters find it remarkably easy to state themselves exactly. Many of his young ladies speak through their appearance—like Mary Thorne, whose face has a "speaking earnestness" (*Doctor Thorne*, 41), or Hetta Carbury, whose face is "a true index of her character" (*The Way We Live Now*, 2). One reason why the Trollopian narrator often complains about the literary necessity of describing his heroine's appearance is that the true narrative of her face is the statement of her character, not an inventory of physical features. Heroes, too, can speak without speech: "'Cora, Cora,'" murmurs the bereaved Plantagenet Palliser, "so that the sense of the sound and not the sound itself had come to him from his own lips" (*The Duke's Children*, 15). Such language is, of course, impossible in the real world, but in the Trollopian world it is common and necessary. Trollope's characters speak the truth without speaking; they and their narrator never balk at the paradox that character is a statement, declared to be nonlanguage only by another statement.

Not only do Trollope's characters emit such unstated statements, but they also read these statements in the world about them. Even the worst of Trollope's unsavory semivillains is able to communicate a good deal without recourse to language:

> All this Mr. Slope read in the slight motion of the bishop's thumb, and he read it correctly. There was no need of parchments and seals, of attestations, explanations, and professions. The bargain was understood between them, and Mr. Slope gave the bishop his hand upon it. The bishop understood the little extra squeeze, and an intelligible gleam of assent twinkled in his eye. (*Barchester Towers*, 18)

One of the most distinctive features of Trollope's characters is the facility with which they are able to read each other's unwritten statements of character. They can sometimes achieve a state of mutual transparency, like that of the Dale sisters in *The Small House at Allington*: "Each of these women understood exactly how the matter stood, and each knew that the other understood it" (6). Such understanding has no need of words; indeed, it often comes about when language is forbidden, or when what is said directly contradicts what is understood. George Vavasor understands his cousin Alice in this style: "'I will marry you,' Alice had said to him,—not in words, but in acts and looks, which were plainer than words" (*Can You Forgive Her?*, 51). Hetta Carbury has a similar insight into her cousin Roger, although in his case behavior seems to contradict truth: "Though he had been slow in speech, she had known since their first meeting how he regarded her! The whole state of his mind had, she had thought, been visible to her,—had been intelligible, gentle, and affectionate" (*The Way We Live Now*, 68). Sometimes intertransparency becomes almost supernatural: Bernard Dale's thoughts about Adolphus Crosbie "threw some sort of shadow across poor Lily's mind, making her feel that her wound was again opened" (*The Small House at Allington*, 33). But usually it is neither remarkable nor surprising when two characters establish the "perfect though not expressed understanding" that Eleanor Harding can enjoy even with Archdeacon Grantly (*The Warden*, 16). Refusal to speak aids sympathy: "Each kept their thoughts to themselves on that subject of which each was thinking; but each sympathised with the other" (*Kept in the Dark*, 16). In this case, refusal of grammar may do its part as well.

There is no essential difference, for Trollope's characters, between the internal listener to whom the discourse of feeling is addressed and the external reader who receives such unwritten messages as these. The same structure exists inside and outside the mind; hearing one's unconscious voice is identical to reading the character of someone else. In both cases, truth is communicated when the message and its emitter are the same, and when this equivalence is also produced in its recipient. Understanding is the agreement of one character statement with another, whether the statements are both in the same mind or transmitted between minds. In this sense, the reader of a Trollope novel perceives truth just as its characters do—judging the agreement of statements that, though some are made within and others between minds, are all in the same language, the same text. The fact that character is said to be neither written nor spoken does not prevent Trollope's characters from reading it. In the same way, the theoretical Trollopian reader reads novels that, except for their minimal taint of plot, are said to be composed of reality, not writing.

Like Trollope's theory, Trollope's novels *describe* the mind and its interaction with other minds as systems of signification, but they *say* that no signification is involved. Signification is confined to conscious discourse, which, like plot in the theory, is admittedly structured like language. Unconscious discourse, the language of the heart, has precisely the same structure, but always attached to it is the neutralizing statement that this signification is not what it is. Feeling is not a comment on character; it is character, and the speaker or writer of it is identical with what he speaks or writes. Character, when it states itself, is not subject to interpretation—an advantage also enjoyed, theoretically, by the text of a realistic novel. One cannot interpret a discourse that is the same as its subject, nor can there be interpretation when the interpreter and the object are identical. The difference of the sign from what it signifies allows interpretation and the proliferation of signs—those things that, in the theory, are confined and neutralized by character, and, in the novels, by the wordless discourse of feeling.

Trollope's characters are accomplished orators, writers, and readers. Their lives, and particularly their loves, operate according to the same rules that govern the novel-machine. The difference is that, for the characters, no such strenuous effort is necessary to eliminate the gaps among writer, reader, and written. Intertextuality need not be suppressed, because in the text world of the Trollopian novel, all characters are the same text, as their world is. Sympathy, the goal at which the novel-machine is aimed, comes more easily to the characters, because for them there is no intervening text to be made transparent. In their world, which the novel-machine generates and fully controls, reality is defined by the same writing that states the characters themselves. The paradoxical unwritten writing that Trollope's theory struggles to maintain in existence can exist in the novels merely by declaration: characters speak non-language, read it, and write it; and the wish that brought the novel-machine into being is fulfilled.

I have described, of course, an ideal or a potential state. Most of Trollope's novels do not assume such wordless language, but chronicle the arduous process of its achievement. In almost all cases the heart does speak, and character almost always gets correctly read, but very often the feat takes hundreds of pages of vain thinking before it is done. Even then, as in the case of Lady Alexandrina, there is no necessary connection between reasoning and truth. The one does not prepare for the other, but thinking is allowed to exhaust itself before feeling can be heard. The speech of feeling is a kind of magic trick, like the magical equivalences in Trollope's theory, and like them it cannot be learned or rehearsed; it must simply be done. The life of the community, however, depends on the performance of this trick. Sympathy is the norm in Trollope's novel world, and though his novels are often concerned with characters who have trouble achieving it, these characters are deviants whose happy endings are their absorption into the community from which they have strayed.

Trollope's quirky political beliefs, for example, are dictated much more by faith in sympathy than by trust in logic. He claims in the *Autobiography* that he is "guilty of no absurdity" in calling himself "an advanced conservative liberal" (253), but he is guilty of eliminating the party distinctions that make politics possible. Just as sensational and antisensational readers turn out to be all realists, just as all oppositions in the theory are also unities, so in politics Trollope would combine all parties into one slow process of development, a universal and unlegislated "tendency towards equality." Indeed, it seems that any political doctrine, any consciously formulated or written program, puts the politician in the same suspect class with poets, romancers, and other misusers of language: "A man who entertains in his mind any political doctrine, except as a means of improving the condition of his fellows, I regard as a political intriguer, a charlatan, and a conjurer,—as one who thinks that, by a certain amount of wary wire-pulling, he may raise himself in the estimation of the world" (253-54). Politics without parties, without doctrines, without disagreement on principles, is no politics at all. Such unanimity can exist only in a society whose members may think they oppose each other but who really, unconsciously, are one. This is the state of writer and reader in Trollope's theory and of character in his fiction. It never was the actual state of England—one reason, perhaps, why Trollope was "altogether the wrong man" for the dismaying actualities of Beverley (260). Parliament has the same goal as realistic novels—producing "the gradual effect of moral teaching and education" (260)—but novels can get there more easily, by simply declaring the goal achieved.

Trollope's politics are antipolitical in the same sense that his novels are antiliterary: legislation ought not to be different from life, any more than fiction ought to be. No politician ought to oppose a measure "simply because it is advocated by another" of his own kind (254); novelists should never write about other novels, only about life. Indeed, Trollope goes so far in the *Autobiography* as to claim that his own "principle" of gradual improvement is "at work throughout" the parliamentary process, though it is "hardly acknowledged" by the advocates of it (254). They are, that is, unconscious Trollopians, though they may tell themselves that they are politicians. Trollope's fictional politicians are at their most useful when, like Phineas Finn, they have attained a condition of sympathetic unconsciousness. In that condition, they are fully sensitive to the feelings that, more than any laws or doctrines, really govern human behavior.

Many of these real feelings—distinguished always from the articulated and therefore unreal thoughts that divide men into parties—are associated with one of Trollope's favorite undefinable terms, "gentleman." Trollope's use of this provocatively ambiguous word has often been discussed;[1] it is simply the ideal Trollopian concept, because it is universally understood but can never be explained: "A man in public life could not do himself a greater injury than by saying in public that commissions in the army or navy, or berths in the Civil Service, should be given exclusively to gentlemen. He would be defied to define the term,—and would fail should he attempt to do so. But he would know what he meant, and so very probably would they who defied him" (*Autobiography*, 34). This passage is part of Trollope's justification of his opposition to competitive examinations as a means of choosing members of the Civil Service. His declared reason for opposing such a system is that it ignores class differences. The real reason—or at least the characteristic Trollopian reason—is that examinations must be written or spoken, while the recognition of a gentleman can only be felt, never put into words.

The concept of the gentleman never becomes conscious—that is, it is never defined in words. Like the statements that make up the discourse of feeling, it is reported only in the form of a simple declaration of truth: "He is (is not) a gentleman." No deductions lead to such a conclusion, and the only evidence needed to verify such a statement is the statement itself. In *The Eustace Diamonds*, for example, Lucy Morris enrages Lord Fawn by accusing him of having said an untruth: "Mr. Greystock is a gentleman. If you say that he is not a gentleman, it is not true" (27). Lord Fawn can cite a specific case of what seems to be Greystock's ungentlemanly behavior, but Lucy can only repeat her statement, even extending it to cover all future cases: "It won't be true" (33). In the end it is Lord Fawn, despite his facts, who relents, while Lucy's unconscious certainty remains unshaken and true.

Trollope's fullest treatment of the question is *The Prime Minister*, which seems to offer some tangible attributes of the gentleman, some signs by which the quality expresses itself. As Mr. Wharton says to his daughter Emily: "I like Arthur Fletcher, because he is a gentleman,—because he is a gentleman of the class to which I belong myself; because he works; because I know all about him so that I can be sure of him; because he had a decent father and mother; because I am safe with him, being quite sure that he will say to me neither awkward things nor impertinent things" (10). Ferdinand Lopez, however, proves that the state of being a gentleman cannot be signified, only felt: "In a sense he was what is called

[1]For example, by Richard Faber in *Proper Stations: Class in Victorian Fiction* (London: Faber & Faber, 1971), pp. 126-45.

a gentleman. He knew how to speak, and how to look, how to use a knife and fork, how to dress himself, and how to walk. But he had not the faintest notion of the feelings of a gentleman" (58). Because Lopez has only signs, without feelings, none of the true gentlemen in *The Prime Minister* hesitates for a moment to decide against him. "He is not worth your notice," says Frank Gresham. "He is simply not a gentleman, and does not know how to behave himself" (34). Mr. Wharton is unequivocally "an old-fashioned English gentleman" (43), and he states the case as clearly as anyone in Trollope's fiction ever does: "in all such matters, my dear, the great thing is like to like" (10). One gentleman recognizes another; no interpretation is necessary.

Recognition of likeness is sympathy; society is governed by the same principles that govern the writing and reading of realistic novels. It might be a peculiarly British notion that the surest principles are those that have never been written down, but it is a peculiarly Trollopian notion that the surest principles cannot be expressed at all. Feelings are the only truth, and feelings do not emit signs of themselves that would have to be interpreted, allowing the possibility of error. Feelings are identical with the statement of them, and statements of feeling are never made in any kind of interpretable language. Signs can be counterfeited, but feelings cannot. Feelings speak, but it is nonspeech; they are read, but it is nonreading. Trollope's theory of fiction is based upon paradoxes like these, and his theory of life makes them the basis of human intercourse on all its levels, from that of a pair of lovers to that of parliamentary legislation.

It makes no difference that in the real world, which Trollope's novels claim to report, nothing is possible without signification and interpretation. Indeed, Trollope's novels are very much concerned with the difficulties that misread signs may cause. But there is in Trollope's novels—as there is not in the real world—an alternative to interpretation, a promise of complete and certain knowledge with no possibility of error. The dream of a language in which no lies can be told—although the possibility of lying is the possibility of language[2]—is dreamt everywhere in Trollope's writing, theory and practice alike. In his theory, the dream is constantly threatened by the realities of writing, and it never quite comes true. But in his novels, where nothing is real except what is written there, the dream is the definition of truth.

[2]In *A Theory of Semiotics* (Bloomington: Indiana University Press, 1976), Umberto Eco defines semiotics as *"in principle the discipline studying everything which can be used in order to lie. If something cannot be used to tell a lie, conversely it cannot be used to tell the truth: it cannot in fact be used 'to tell' at all"* (p. 7).

Even within the Trollopian dream world, however, the achievement of uninterpretable truth can have some strenuous and unpleasant consequences, particularly for the marriageable young ladies who are Trollope's most famous character type. "It is admitted," declares the *Autobiography*, "that a novel can hardly be made interesting or successful without love" (192)—another requirement imposed by reality on an unwilling novelist, who so totally accepts it that his one attempt to write a novel without love "breaks down before the conclusion" (162). Most of Trollope's novels contain at least one young lady in love, and many of them have several. His dutiful obedience of this supposed rule allows him to sum up his whole career as "the fabrication of love-stories" (294). I have shown in several cases that the *Autobiography* most clearly describes the internal necessities of the novel-machine when it says that they are external impositions. The same is true in this case: love, and particularly feminine love, is the novel-machine's favorite subject, chosen by it just as willfully as it chooses not to write about poetical flights and romantic adventures. In a world where nothing but interpersonal relations is real, no doubt love would have special importance. In a world where sympathy is the highest good, the intense sympathy of love would naturally rank high. And in a world where the value of a feeling is inversely proportional to its ease of articulation, the traditional irrationality of love would certainly make it valuable. Yet none of these factors explains the peculiar structure of Trollopian love and the peculiar problems it sometimes creates for the young ladies who fall into it.

Most of my examples of the double discourse of the Trollopian mind were taken from descriptions of young female minds engaged in thoughts about love. The male mind is an altogether sloppier organ than the female, in Trollope's psychology. Men are much more likely than women to become permanently entangled in thinking, and even the wickedest of Trollope's men are saved from outright villainy by the inadvertence with which they lead themselves into evil. Trollope's women think very little. This, however, is a virtue, since they are proportionately adept at feeling, and they are generally in close touch with the unconscious voice that speaks only truth. They are easily able to achieve the equivalence between listener and speaker, thought and feeling, that produces true statements of character. And the truest statement a Trollopian woman can make —spoken, written, or only thought—is the declaration that she loves some man. Indeed, Trollope's women often make such statements very early in their fictional careers. They are seldom involved, as his men often are, in long courses of mental debate that lead to truth only after several hundred pages of thoughtful vacillation. Yet the declaration of love, once made, does not guarantee contentment. For some of Trollope's young ladies, the consequences of declaring their love are far more arduous than the preparations they make for declaring it. Trollope's women suffer, sometimes severely, from the consequences of love. They do so not because such consequences have been dictated to the novelist by the world, but because love is Trollope's favorite metaphor for what the novelist does and what novels ought to be.

If one were to follow the advice of the *Autobiography*, taking the behavior of Trollope's fictional young ladies as a model for the behavior of real-life girls "when lovers come" (189), one would conclude that Trollope's novels recommend a refreshing degree of frankness. As the *Autobiography* remarks, commenting on *Framley Parsonage:* "it was downright honest love, — in which there was no pretence on the part of the lady that she was too ethereal to be fond of a man, no half-and-half inclination on the part of the man to pay a certain price and no more for a pretty toy. Each of them longed for the other, and they were not ashamed to say so" (123-24). Such praise of openness is frequent in the novels. "She threw from her, at once, as vain and wicked and false, all idea of coying her love," says the narrator of *The Eustace Diamonds* about Lucy Morris (15), using a form of the peculiarly Trollopian verb "to coy," which may have been Trollope's invention. Similarly praise-worthy clarity marks Lily Dale's behavior early in *The Small House at Allington:* "She had seen girls who were half ashamed of their love; but she would never be ashamed of hers or of him. She had given herself to him; and now all the world might know it, if all the world cared for such knowledge. Why should she be ashamed of that which, to her thinking, was so great an honour to her?" (9). Once they have heard the voice of feeling, Trollope's women are unembarrassed to repeat its message. The message is a true statement of what they are, and there can be no reason for coyness about such unambiguous, uninterpretable truth.

The cases of Lucy Morris and Lily Dale, however, illustrate another distinctive feature of Trollopian love, one that oddly qualifies Trollope's hearty praise of frankness. Lucy has "given her heart—for good and all, as she owned to herself—to Frank Greystock," but she has done so with no assurance from him that her love is returned: "She had given away her heart, and yet she would do without a lover" (3). For most of the novel, Lucy steadfastly waits, asserting her trust in Frank against all evidence of his dalliance with Lizzie Eustace. Her steadfastness is praised as highly as her openness, but there is in it the curious implication that, once a woman has stated her love, that statement remains in force whether or not the world provides a referent for it. The implication is fully explored, and carried to the conclusion of its own logic, in the career of Lily Dale, which begins in *The Small House at Allington* and ends in *The Last Chronicle of Barset*. Lily is jilted by the man to whom she has given her heart, and no amount of persuasion will bring her to revise a statement that has steadily less and less to do with the reality of the world around her. Indeed, by jilting her, Crosbie has proven himself to be other than the man Lily loves, but she remains till the end obstinately devoted to a love that never had, and never will have, a real object. The narrator of *The Last Chronicle*, evidently relieved, dismisses her with the assurance, "in this last word I shall ever write respecting her, that she will live and die as Lily Dale" (77), and the *Autobiography* regards her popularity with readers as a perversity, calling her "a female prig" (154). Lily's popularity might have been due to the perversity of readers, but the perversity of her career is Trollope's own. She carries to an extreme the implications that are always latent in the discourse of feeling: it is absolutely true, always was and always will be true, and no character has the power to alter a statement that does not express but *is* himself.

Truth of statement and truth to one's love are the same for Trollope's young women. They commonly agree with Lady Frances Trafford in *Marion Fay:* "When a girl has once brought herself to tell a man that she loves him, according to my idea she cannot give him up" (12). Lady Mary Palliser has the same idea in *The Duke's Children:* "She had told the man that she loved him, and after that there could be no retreat" (5). Emily Hotspur concurs, "My love was a thing to give, but when given I cannot take it back" (*Sir Harry Hotspur of Humblethwaite*, 8). In Emily's case, this common assumption has the uncommon consequence of a long course of devotional reading followed by death. Like Lily Dale, she has declared her love to an unworthy man but refuses to change her mind. Unlike Lily, she never settles into spinsterhood, but dies of sheer self-consistency. Trollope's novels assume absolute fidelity as the precondition of any female love statement. Given this assumption, the novels portray a great number of possible consequences, each different from the others according to the degree to which external reality does or does not correspond to what the heart has said. Most often, after a series of trials, the woman is brought together with her chosen man. In a few instances, however, reality refuses to provide an equivalent of what the heart has named. These circumstances do not change the structure of love or the truth of the lover's statement; they merely guarantee that the lover will always be at odds with the world that ought to have welcomed her. Even in Emily Wharton's case, though her chosen man has been universally recognized as a blackguard, and run over by a train, the effort to rectify the mistake of loving him leaves her "warped from herself" (*The Prime Minister*, 74). In the end, she does marry Arthur Fletcher, but she is persuaded to do so only by his tepidly reasonable argument: "You are one of us, and should do as all of us wish you. If, indeed, you could not love me it would be different" (79).

These few cases of love gone wrong have the look of experiments, speculations on the possible results of adherence to a premise. They are extreme instances of the obstinacy to which most of Trollope's characters are given in a milder degree, a dogged devotion to the truth of their own natures. I will discuss this peculiarly Trollopian characteristic more fully in the next chapter. It is apparent, however, that for women in love, the inner equivalence that allows feeling to speak takes precedence over the outer reality to which that speech is addressed. Feeling comes first. So long as it is blocked or delayed by thinking, it may remain only an unconscious mumble; but once it takes hold of language—once the internal speaker and listener merge into a statement that can be given to the world—feeling speaks with absolute authority, regardless of thought and even of fact. Ordinarily in the Trollopian world, truth of feeling is met by understanding. Often, indeed, the meeting is easily arranged. But when Trollope's women announce their love, the announcement is true only of their feelings. It is fully possible for them to love a man who never existed, and to remain forever devoted to an imagined lover. The love is true whether or not it has an object; the statement of love is true because it is its own referent.

Perfect understanding is achieved between Trollopian lovers when the idea in each lover's mind is matched by the reality of the other. The idea may be, as it is for Lizzie Eustace, an absurd idea of swashbuckling heroism that no real man can live up to. Or it may be, as it is for Lily Dale and Emily Hotspur, the mistaken idea that a certain real man deserves to be loved. Or the idea may be correct, as it is for Lucy Morris and the majority of Trollope's young ladies. But, though the idea is directed outward as expectation, and though no Trollopian character attains happiness through imagination alone, the imagination has always conceived of a lover before any real lover proves himself. Love is not mimetic: statements of love are statements of character, and as such they are true only of their speakers, not their addressees. Trollope's women do not fall in love with their men because the men are lovable; they do so because they recognize in their men something inexpressible that exactly corresponds to their idea. Ideal love is always true; its statement is "I love what I love." Real love, however, which depends on interpretation as ideal love does not, has always the potential of error, failure to match the

ideal. There is no guarantee that the idea of love will find its real equivalent, and when the equivalence does happen, it has all the magical quality
of those other equivalences in Trollope's theory—reader and character,
novelist and reader, fiction and reality—that occur without imitation or
the intervention of signs. Love is always ideal to begin with; it may or
may not be realized.

The structure of Trollopian love is illustrated at greatest length in
one of Trollope's last novels, *Ayala's Angel*. This complex and light-
hearted novel contains a great number of love matches—so many, indeed,
that its narrator can boast about the neatness of their arrangement (64)
—but the most interesting one, from which the novel takes its title, is that
between Ayala Dormer and Colonel Jonathan Stubbs. Ayala starts out
with all the misconceptions that lead Lizzie Eustace to disaster: her
"somewhat romantic name" reflects the "poetic charm" and "taste for
romance" with which she is graced and handicapped (1); she is "romantic,
dreamy, poetic, childish" (7); she is "full of romance and nonsense, and
isn't half as fond of telling the truth as she ought to be" (13); worst of all,
as Mrs. Dossett remarks, she is "romantic, which is very objectionable"
(13). Ayala is burdened with a "theory of life" (5), which she has assembled
from scraps of "poetry and novels and trash" (39). Like Lizzie, she has
drastically misread such writing, taking it to be a guide to life when only
realistic writing can serve that purpose. Like Lizzie, she expects the real
world to produce for her a lover out of poems—an Angel who, like
Lizzie's Corsair, exists nowhere except in poetry. But, unlike Lizzie, Ayala
can be saved. Her romantic name also implies that poetry is a dream
from which she can awake; there are faculties in her that are only dormant
and that can be activated. The story of Ayala Dormer is a unique instance
in Trollope's novels of education in correct reading. Her step-by-step
progress away from romance, into realism, runs the full length of *Ayala's*
Angel. It is Trollope's most extensive portrait of how the mind ought to
read itself, the world, and realistic fiction.

The Angel for whom Ayala waits is her own creation. Unlike Lizzie's
Corsair, whom in her imaginative poverty she lifts whole out of Byron,
Ayala's Angel has been assembled from bits and pieces of various poems.
His characteristics are vague: he has "wings tinged with azure"; he is
"transcendental, more than human" (6); he inhabits some ethereal "castle-
in-the-air" (10). He resembles Shelley more than anyone else, but he is
"confined altogether to the abstract," a "conception of poetic perfection"
in which there is "not as yet any appanage of apparel, of features, or of
wealth" (6). The most distinctive feature of the Angel is his absence; no
real man has, at first, anything of the Angel about him. During the first

quarter of the novel, Ayala is approached by several would-be suitors, all of whom are nonangelic. She sees several love matches forming around her, but though real presence will do for others, Ayala reserves unreal absence for herself:

> Isadore Hamel would, of course, come again, and would, of course, marry Lucy . . . and then—then—in the far distance, something else would come, something of which in her castle-building she had not yet developed the form, of which she did not yet know the bearing, or the manner of its beauty, or the music of its voice; but as to which she was very sure that its form would be beautiful and its voice full of music. . . . It was the extreme point of perfection at which she would arrive at last, when her thoughts had become sublimated by the intensity of her thinking. It was the tower of the castle from which she could look down upon the inferior world below,—the last point of the dream in arranging which she would all but escape from earth to heaven,—when in the moment of her escape the cruel waking back into the world would come upon her. (10)

Everything about the Angel is unreal, unspecified, impossible; but one thing is sure: though Ayala knows nothing about how he looks, she knows exactly how she feels about him. The feeling never changes, and Ayala's certainty of it never wavers. Her reformation does not change her feeling; it merely provides an object.

During the course of the novel, in a typically Trollopian process of gradual clarification, Ayala learns to equip her Angel with all the attributes that he does "not yet" have at the start. Again she is imaginative, even artistic. Working within the preexisting outlines of her feeling —which, like character in Trollope's theory, is always already there and always stays the same—she steadily works to fill in the blanks, to make the absent Angel present by giving him real characteristics. Like language for the novelist, "the colours with which he is to paint his picture," these characteristics do nothing to feeling but convey it. They make Ayala's feeling "intelligible," as the novelist's characters should be, "intelligible without trouble" (*Autobiography*, 201). When Ayala first meets Jonathan Stubbs, he seems to be even less angelic than the other real men who have failed her test. He is, at first, the contradiction of the Angel: "Nothing could be more unlike an Angel of Light than Colonel Stubbs" (16). But as the Angel gradually turns real, his characteristics are always found to be those that Stubbs already possesses. Ayala goes from maintaining that Stubbs's manner is "altogether unlike that of a lover" (23) to the admission that Stubbs is not a wholly unangelic name and that the Angel might have Stubbsian red hair (26). The real man who begins as the opposite of the Angel of Light is gradually allowed to have "something of the Angel about him" (45), then "no more than a few of the real atrributes of an

Angel of Light" (49), and finally "all those attributes which should by right belong to an Angel of Light" (52)—at which point Ayala discovers that the real object of her feeling has been Jonathan Stubbs all along:

> That he was tender and true, manly, heroic,—as brightly angelic as could be any Angel of Light,—was already an absolute fact to her. No!—her heart had never been predisposed to any one else. It was of him she had always dreamed even long before she had seen him. He was the man, perfect in all good things, who was to come and take her with him—if ever man should come and take her. (52)

In the last sentence of the novel, Ayala is handed over, "to her own intense satisfaction," to her real "ANGEL OF LIGHT" (64).

The desire that is satisfied by marriage has not changed since the first page of the novel. It is Ayala's truth, her character—for Ayala, as for Trollope's women generally, character is a statement of need. Poetry and romance have taught Ayala to figure her need in false and impossible terms, but Trollopian realism teaches her its downright honest figures. "I knew how to love you," she tells her real Angel, "but I did not know how to tell you that I loved you" (56). The eventual Angel, Jonathan Stubbs, is a thoroughly Trollopian figure. He is "one of the very few who always know what to do at the moment without taking time to think of it" (45); he is "chiefly given to poetry, tobacco, and military matters" (19), and he knows the proper place for all such pastimes, especially poetry. "I don't mind a little Byron now and again," he tells Isadore Hamel, "so there is no nonsense" (18). He is "a man of the earth really" (49), who has his own dream lover, but one that corresponds exactly to what is real: "I dream that she does scold so awfully when I have her to myself. In my dreams, you know, I'm married to her, and she always wants me to eat hashed mutton. Now, if there is one thing that makes me more sick than another it is hashed mutton. Of course I shall marry her in some of my waking moments, and then I shall have to eat hashed mutton for ever" (23). In exchanging her castles in the air for the hashed-mutton dreams of Jonathan Stubbs, Ayala learns that poetry belongs on the drawing room table. But she also learns the more important lesson, the supreme Trollopian lesson, that happiness comes when dreams and reality speak the same language. Her desire meets its satisfaction when she masters the distinctively Trollopian feat of dreaming the real.

The structure of Ayala's mind is the same as that of Trollope's other heroines, and her love has the same double-edged power of unalterable certainty. When she finally becomes aware that she loves Jonathan Stubbs, she discovers that she has always loved him. Her desire has never changed, but only found at last the proper words in which to state itself. This same permanence of character statement, this love by definition, leads Lily Dale to spinsterhood and Emily Hotspur to death; but the real world provides the right words for Ayala, and she is able to state herself fully in terms of a real man. *Ayala's Angel* is Trollope's most detailed portrayal of how the mind and its world can become the same; it is the romance of realistic writing. In that other romance, the story of Anthony Trollope in the *Autobiography*, a young man also finds the real world deficient and supplements his unsatisfied desire with castles in the air. For Anthony, as for Ayala, the desire never changes; and for both of them satisfaction is achieved when dreams find real language in which to state themselves. Ayala, however, is a creature of the text, and her love can be completely satisfied by another such creature, whose text is the same as her own. Anthony, a living man, takes a detour through fiction: his desire is always left just short of satisfaction, limited by plot, by publication, by the many imperfections in the novel-making process that announce that the world is different from his dreams. Unlike Ayala, Anthony is always displaced from satisfaction, and so he constructs a machine for reducing the gap—a paradoxical device powered by the very difference that it intends to erase.

What Trollope's novels call "love" his theory calls "novels," and the tragedy of Anthony Trollope's story is that though love can be written, writing can never be love. When Trollope lays aside his identity and begins to write novels, he gives up forever the possibility of real satisfaction, taking in its place the privilege of always writing about it. The novel-machine is engaged for all its life in a voluminous declaration of love to a real world that can never respond. The very mechanism that makes the declaration guarantees the absence of an answer, though it writes more than anything else about answers found and satisfaction achieved. If an answer ever came, there would be no need for novels.

The structure of love in Trollope's fiction is the same as the ideal structure of writing and reading in his theory. Love may have come first in Trollope's life, or perhaps writing did; but in his novels love achieves what in his theory writing ought to do—a state of equivalence between imagination and reality, fiction and fact. That writing is always different gives the theory its paradoxes and contradictions, but it keeps the machine running. That writing is always different keeps the novelist perpetually unsatisfied, and perpetually writing. In the end, Trollope's realism, like any idealism, is the dream of a world in which no dreams are necessary, and no novel-machines need ever be devised.

Writing Madness

He Knew He Was Right

SO FAR, I have followed the *Autobiography* in treating the world of Trollope's novels as a single world, unaffected by the divisions imposed upon it by the necessities of writing and publication. The novelist's life with his characters is carried on independently of such divisions. The reader should theoretically duplicate that experience, and the novels themselves put beginnings and endings in the artificial realm of writing, not in the real world. The Barsetshire and Palliser series, along with the recurrence of earlier characters in later novels, reinforce this impression. Trollope had no such grand design as the *Comédie humaine*, but his novels constitute one world, one earth hewn into literary pieces. The Trollopian way of surveying his output as a whole would be, like his figures for character, metonymic: each novel is a zone of the same real earth, an area of the same written canvas, and the structure of any particular novel is unimportant by comparison with the total structure to which each novel contributes a part. The anti-Trollopian way, which I will take in this chapter, is to analyze in one novel, *He Knew He Was Right*, the subtle system of internal divisions that, like Trollope's rhetoric in general, aims at (and achieves) the impression that the novel has no internal divisions, and no rhetoric.

So far, I have also followed the *Autobiography* in treating Trollope's theory and fiction as independent of his life. The *Autobiography* declares this distinction on its first page, and though it discusses the novels generally in the order of their writing, it never suggests that the order of writing has anything to do with the nature of the fictional world. That world has its own chronology, which runs parallel to the chronology of Anthony Trollope's life, and one would learn nothing from the coincidence that a fictional event was written down at the time of some real event in the writer's insignificant career. Trollope's theory precludes any inquiry into "development," any lining up of the novels in the accidental order of their writing to see whether they or their writer changed with the passing of actual time. Each novel is a brush stroke on a single canvas, and the order of brush strokes has nothing to do with the portrait. Perhaps Trollope's novels together make a "plot," perhaps that plot is intertwined with the plot of his life; but to valorize such things, even if they exist, would be as anti-Trollopian as to value the plot of a novel above its portrayal of character. It is anti-Trollopian to make the following declaration: *He Knew He Was Right* is an especially significant novel in the plot of Trollope's life; the nature of the novel and its place in Trollope's career are, in spite of the theory, vitally related.

Trollope's artistic development has been a problem for literary critics, because he seems not to have had any worthy of comment. His first three novels show signs of uncertainty, as if he were groping about for a method; but starting with *The Warden*, and culminating with *Framley Parsonage*, he seems to have devised a way of writing fiction to which he adhered without significant change until he died. There are occasional detours and lapses, but these are distributed throughout Trollope's career, and no intelligible pattern can be made of them. Trollope seems to have found his method early, and, like his own theoretical novel-machine, he seems to have gone on making novels in the same way until the end. Most critics who have attacked this problem, though they have failed to discover a satisfactory pattern in the whole of Trollope's output, have agreed that, within the apparent continuum, the late 1860s mark a zone of change. A.O.J. Cockshut locates there the inauguration of the "progress towards pessimism" that leads to the "dark" novels of the 1870s.[1] John E. Dustin finds there a time of "fatigue" with the "thematic alternation" of Trollope's first twenty years as a novelist.[2] For William Cadbury, the late 1860s saw a shift from Trollope's earlier affinities with epic to his later dabbling in romance.[3] Gordon Ray sees in those years the emergence of a

---

[1] *Anthony Trollope: A Critical Study* (New York: New York University Press, 1968), p. 131.

[2] "Thematic Alternation in Trollope," *PMLA* 77 (1962): 283.

[3] "Shape and Theme: Determinants of Trollope's Forms," *PMLA* 78 (1963): 329.

new interest in "the darker aspects of life and character," stimulated by the criticisms of R. H. Hutton and others.[4] And James R. Kincaid finds between 1867 and 1875 a series of "variations in irony" characterized by a sense of "an uncertain focus, of a shifting focus, or of none at all."[5] No critic has provided a single line of development that would account for the totality of Trollope's fiction, but all such attempts have remarked that some sort of turn, or change, or crisis happened in the years about 1870.

The *Autobiography* records a provocative cluster of disruptions in those years. In 1867, Trollope resigns from the Post Office, giving up the parallel career to which he had always devoted "more unflagging attention" than to the writing of novels (243). In the same year, he takes on the editorship of the *St. Paul's Magazine*, a financial failure from which he resigns in 1870. In the fall of 1868, he runs unsuccessfully for Parliament, and in 1871 he leaves his well-loved home at Waltham Cross on account of "questions as to expense" (294). By the spring of 1871, he is considering the abandonment of hunting—another parallel career that "neither the writing of books, nor the work of the Post Office, nor other pleasures" has been able to restrict (55)—and at the same time he first faces the prospect that "at fifty-five I ought to give up the fabrication of love-stories" (294). There is little obvious evidence in the novels Trollope writes during this time to suggest any radical change, though in 1865 and 1866 he tries the curious experiment of anonymously publishing *Nina Balatka* and *Linda Tressel*, "in order that I might see whether I could succeed in obtaining a second identity" (175). The experiment is a reasonable success, at least as far as the anonymity goes, but in 1867 Trollope takes the more drastic step of laying aside his familiar identity forever, by means of the unequivocally titled *Last Chronicle of Barset*. In 1870, he publishes his translation of Caesar's *Commentaries*, for which he receives no payment, though the critical reception of "this soaring out of my own peculiar line" still rankles when the *Autobiography* is written (291). And the structure of the *Autobiography* marks 1867 as an unexplained watershed, inserting between its discussions of *Linda Tressel* and the *Last Chronicle* three chapters of theory and criticism, then picking up the narrative of Trollope's life after a sixty-page interruption as if nothing had intervened.

There is sufficient biographical evidence that some sort of crisis afflicted Trollope in the late 1860s and early 1870s, but the crisis is so

---

[4] "Trollope at Full Length," *Huntington Library Quarterly* 31 (1968): 329.
[5] *The Novels of Anthony Trollope* (Oxford: Clarendon Press, 1977), p. 144.

peculiar, so Trollopian, that one can make little use of the evidence to locate anything like a turning point in his career. Trollope's career did not turn; instead, the multiple identities of his life—novel writing, Post Office work, hunting, family and social life—were shifted and exchanged. Some old identities were discarded, other new ones were taken on, still others were doubled or remodeled. Multiplication of identity, the maintenance of plurality within unity, is as characteristic of Trollope's life as multiple plots are of his fiction. From the moment when he lays his identity aside and becomes a novelist, there is no longer an entity called Anthony Trollope to which any change in his art or behavior could be traced back as to a single source. The novelist is always doubled, a living man and a liver-with his characters; and each of those identities is internally doubled and doubled again, producing not so much a single character as a battalion of independent functions, each of which proceeds on its course without invading the others. Like Trollope's multiply plotted novels, which are organized in much the same way, his multiply plotted life is nevertheless a unity despite its inner diversity. But neither the novels nor the life offers an unequivocal center to which all else might be subordinated or referred.

There is one other real-life event of the late 1860s, however, that deserves special attention. The time that I have called Trollope's "crisis" was also the time of his greatest popular and financial success. The watershed year, as Michael Sadleir calls it, was 1869, when *Phineas Finn* and *He Knew He Was Right* were published.[6] For each of these novels, Trollope received £3200, more money than he was ever again to get for a single work. Neither of them repaid its investment, and the failure of the latter brought about the bankruptcy of Virtue & Co., which was also financing the unsuccessful *St. Paul's Magazine* with Trollope as editor. The decline in Trollope's earning power did not become serious until after 1875, when the melancholy footnote was added to the *Autobiography*, recording his "diminution in price" (138). But Trollope's two novels of 1869 exceed his own standard, decided upon in 1870, of £600 for an "ordinary novel volume" and £3000 for "a long tale published in twenty parts, which is equal in length to five such volumes" (138). The difference between £3200 and £3000 is perhaps insignificant financially —it certainly ought to have no literary significance—yet *He Knew He Was Right* marks Trollope's encounter with a real-life limit that may have been waiting for him all along. The novel was an excess. The world was not willing to pay for it at the anticipated rate, and it pushed

[6]*Anthony Trollope: A Commentary* (Boston: Houghton Mifflin, 1927), p. 291.

Trollope's output for 1869 beyond even the "fecundity of the herring" displayed by the mythical novelist in the *Autobiography* who turned out three three-volume novels in a year. It would be too much to claim that Trollope's "crisis" of the late 1860s simply caused the excessiveness of *He Knew He Was Right*. Yet excess is the greatest threat to the novel-machine, and *He Knew He Was Right* was the first clear evidence in Trollope's career that he had finally gone too far. The novel also disrupted the easy translation of writing into money and money into real life, on which, in Trollope's theory, the novelist's existence depends.

The failure of *He Knew He Was Right* in the literary marketplace was no doubt due in part to the weariness of the reading public with the sheer quantity of Trollope's fiction. In his "Partial Portrait," Henry James admits that after *He Knew He Was Right*—though it was "good enough to encourage a continuance of favours, as the shopkeepers say"—he had ceased to keep up with Trollope's steady output.[7] James's dismay might well have been shared by many readers; no matter what sort of novel it had been, it would probably have failed. To make matters worse, it is a "very long novel," the only one of Trollope's novels about whose length even the *Autobiography* complains (275). And it is an uncharacteristic work from the chronicler of Barsetshire, a somber, bitter tale of petty insanity. Until recent years, critics have had nothing good to say about it, calling it a "total anomaly" in Trollope's career,[8] dismissing it as a "mediocre 'dark' novel,"[9] joining the *Autobiography* in its judgment that the novel is "nearly altogether bad" (276).[10] There is some irony in the notion that *He Knew He Was Right* may have been another effort on Trollope's part to win a new "identity" for himself, to appropriate areas of experience that lay apparently beyond the borders of Barsetshire. Those areas were the preserve of Trollope's constant antagonists, the sensation novelists, and *He Knew He Was Right* is a clear case of the flirtation with sensationalism that I have discussed in chapter 5. The flirtation did not begin with *He Knew He Was Right*, nor did it end there; but the novel may mark the point at which the sensation novel ceased to be an opponent in the real world of novel readers and took up permanent residence inside the novel-machine.

[7]Reprinted in *Trollope: The Critical Heritage*, ed. Donald Smalley (London: Routledge & Kegan Paul, 1969), p. 537.

[8]Dustin, "Thematic Alternation," p. 283.

[9]Ray, "Trollope at Full Length," p. 333.

[10]The novel receives appreciative attention in Cockshut, *Trollope*, pp. 169-79; in Kincaid, *Novels of Anthony Trollope*, pp. 149-55; and in Ruth apRoberts, "Emily and Nora and Dorothy and Priscilla and Jemima and Carry," in *The Victorian Experience: The Novelists*, ed. Richard Levine (Athens: Ohio University Press, 1976), pp. 87-120.

As T.H.S. Escott was the first to observe, the Barsetshire novels had been primarily "comedy narrative," while in the mid-1860s Trollope began to produce novels that belong "more or less to melodrama."[11] This change, according to Escott, was the result of Trollope's desire to conform to the "literary tendencies" of the time. In *He Knew He Was Right*, desire had intensified into "anxiety to convince the public that he had as keen an eye as ever for the very newest actualities" of contemporary life.[12] Only a few years earlier, in 1862, Trollope had successfully performed just such a maneuver, exploiting in *Orley Farm* the sensational subjects of forgery and female criminality. At that time, however, the sensation novel was a new phenomenon, and its subjects still had the appeal of novelty. By 1869, the sensation novel had already come close to wearing itself out; its heavy concentration on a small number of topics and a smaller number of narrative tricks had quickly deprived them of whatever shock value they might once have had. If Trollope intended to win over readers from the sensational camp by offering them a novel about madness, he made a serious misjudgment about what would sell. *He Knew He Was Right*, considered simply as a book about a madman, would more likely have had the reverse effect—convincing readers that Trollope, who had been grinding out novels for more than twenty years, was hopelessly passé.

Madness is far from the only subject of *He Knew He Was Right*, and even at that it is a peculiarly Trollopian kind of madness, which has more to do with the novel-machine than with any sort of derangement in the real world. But madness had long been a favorite device of sensational fiction, and it had made the fortune of more than one clever hack. Madness is Lady Audley's secret; it appears frequently in the other works turned out in the 1860s by Miss Braddon, J. S. LeFanu, Mrs. Wood, and others. As early as 1866, the *Saturday Review* found that Mrs. Wood's latest novel, *St. Martin's Eve*, failed to produce the sensations it tried for because "madness pure and simple, as an element in sensation novels," had already become "rather stale."[13] In the same year William Gilbert, who had attracted some attention in 1863 with *Shirley Hall Asylum, or The Memoirs of a Monomaniac*, turned in *Dr. Austin's Guests* to what one reviewer was able to call "the whimsical side of insanity."[14] Such sensational madness is, of course, chiefly a device for arranging thrilling revelations and excusing the inconceivable behavior that a convoluted

[11] *Anthony Trollope: His Work, Associates, and Literary Originals* (London: John Lane, 1913), p. 205.
[12] Ibid., p. 293.
[13] Review of *St. Martin's Eve, Saturday Review* 21 (31 March 1866): 387.
[14] Review of *Dr. Austin's Guests, Saturday Review* 22 (29 December 1866): 798.

plot may require. Louis Trevelyan's madness in *He Knew He Was Right* is nothing so expedient. But even if Trollope intended, as he had done in *Orley Farm*, to dignify a sensational trick by giving it realistic treatment, he miscalculated the interest that readers would be likely to feel in such a project, no matter how brilliantly it was carried out.

Contemporary reviewers found *He Knew He Was Right* to be an unexpectedly dour novel, but typical of Trollope in one respect, its shortage of plot. According to *The Times*, the novel is "shapeless as a boned fowl, entirely without any skeleton of plot or incident."[15] It may seem to modern readers, on the contrary, that *He Knew He Was Right* has more plot than is usual for Trollope, since the progress of Trevelyan's madness, acted out mentally and spatially, gives the novel an accelerating forward drive not present in Trollope's more placid works. This on-goingness, this movement from event to event, is implied in the term "plot" as the *Autobiography* uses it, since such movement follows the direction of writing and reading. This is not the kind of "plot," however, that would give a novel a skeleton, a recognizable pattern of articulation. For this other kind of plot, which *He Knew He Was Right* indeed fails to provide in the sense exemplified by Wilkie Collins, the *Autobiography* devises a different figure.

Along with its advice to the beginning novelist on such oratorical matters as "harmony" and "rhythm," the *Autobiography* defines a novel's structure in spatial terms borrowed from painting:

> Though his story should be all one, yet it may have many parts. Though the plot itself may require but few characters, it may be so enlarged as to find its full development in many. There may be subsidiary plots, which shall all tend to the elucidation of the main story, and which will take their places as part of one and the same work, —as there may be many figures on a canvas which shall not to the spectator seem to form themselves into separate pictures. (205)

This is "proportion." It is the reverse of the painter's art, since he "suits the size of his canvas to his subject," while the novelist is told by the real world that he must fill a certain number of pages or volumes and he must "teach himself so to tell his story that it shall naturally fall into the required length" (204-5). The result, however, is still a painting—a curious sort of painting that produces its canvas as the paint is laid down. Again, where Trollope seems to mold his art to external requirements, he actually makes that art self-generating. The implication is that, starting with any thread or fragment of "the plot itself," the novelist can indefinitely amplify

---

[15] *The Times*, 26 August 1869, p. 4; reprinted in *Critical Heritage*, p. 329.

and multiply it, arriving at its "full development" whenever he chooses to get there.

Multiple plotting is a characteristic feature of Victorian novels in general, and particularly of Trollope's. Trollope, indeed, has often been censured for his typical method, and often in terms like these of T.H.S. Escott:

> Trollope, therefore, consistently and to the last, in the structure of his novels persevered with a method somewhat apt to try his readers' patience. In other words, by distracting attention from the creatures of his imagination originally placed in the foreground, he weakens their hold upon the mind. The legitimate or the most serviceable purpose of an underplot is to illustrate from another part of the stage, or on a stage entirely different, those evolutions of character or courses of action belonging to the maiden narrative. This was almost . . . entirely ignored by Trollope.[16]

Bradford Booth finds it "tragic" that Trollope never learned to write a "clean, bare narrative," but insisted upon "cluttering up" his novels with "irrelevant subplots."[17] And A.O.J. Cockshut finds it "strange" that the "subplot" of *Mr. Scarborough's Family* "seems to weaken" the main plot.[18] Recent critics have found subtler strategies in Trollope's multiple plotting,[19] but disparaging comments were common in Trollope's day as well, and the *Autobiography* seems to invite them by suggesting that an enterprising novelist may take any tiny idea and pad it out to any size. Yet the *Autobiography* also maintains that such padding is not imported from outside "the plot itself," but generated by that plot in the process of its "full development." The novel as a whole can, therefore, hardly help being "all one," since it tells only one story, however many parts the story may contain.

The real-life requirements of pages and volumes are not the novelist's goal, as if he began with a deficient little tale and supplemented it. Rather, those requirements set a limit on the expansion of which any "plot" is capable. It is in keeping with the economy of the novel-machine, which pits the expansion of language against the nonlinguistic limits of reality, that each novel produced by the machine should display an equilibrium of extensive and intensive energies. The "plot itself" shares the incon-

---

[16]*Anthony Trollope*, p. 304.

[17]*Anthony Trollope: Aspects of His Life and Art* (Bloomington: Indiana University Press, 1958), p. 121.

[18]*Trollope*, p. 151.

[19]There is a provocative discussion of Trollope's "theory of multiple structure," concentrating on his indebtedness to the Elizabethan and Jacobean dramatists, in Robert Tracy, *Trollope's Later Novels* (Berkeley: University of California Press, 1978), pp. 32-69. The subject is also briefly treated in Kincaid, *Novels of Anthony Trollope*, pp. 30-32.

tinence that Trollope's theory attributes to writing in general. Plot cannot limit itself; it requires the imposed limits of the "canvas" to keep it from developing indefinitely. That canvas is character, reality. It is the one thing that binds plot to the real world, that guarantees that the novelist will not soar into wordy spaces as poets do but will write reality and not just words. Yet the canvas comes into being at the same time as its paint, generating its boundaries with the same gesture that threatens to exceed them.

There is another implication in Trollope's deceptively simple figure for the "proportion" of a novel. If all of a novel's "subsidiary plots" are generated by "the plot itself," if nothing but the limits of a novel's development is imposed from without, then there is no justification for cutting a novel into pieces, abstracting one story line or another from it and regarding the rest of the book as supplemental or subordinate to that "main story." The "meaning" of a Trollope novel—if, indeed, such an autonomous entity can have the subservient function of meaning anything at all—is coincident with the novel itself, in its entirety. Meaning does not reside in part of the novel; it cannot be captured in a plot summary. Only when the reader has seen the entire canvas with all its parts can he judge what its meaning is, and by then he is already outside the novel, loose again in the reality about which the novel is supposed to have taught him and to which he is now supposed to apply what he has learned. In any case, the novel is not supposed to have *meant* life, to have pointed to life like a sign; it is supposed to have *been* life, a circumscribed piece of it, absorbed into the reader's character as any other experience of reality would be. One cannot dissect a Trollope novel without murdering it, one cannot search for its meaning without distorting it, one cannot make the novel signify anything but itself. Like their author, as the *Autobiography* claims, Trollope's novels are "insignificant."

He Knew He Was Right clearly exhibits the built-in expansiveness that the *Autobiography* ascribes to plot, and also the distracting discursiveness that has annoyed many of Trollope's critics. Its first two chapters are devoted to "Shewing How Wrath Began," introducing the "main plot" of the Trevelyans and their quarrel. In addition to the Trevelyans, the "few characters" whom this plot requires are the philandering Colonel Osborne, whose relations with Emily Trevelyan are supposedly improper, and Emily's sister Nora, who acts as her confidante. In chapter 3, a few paragraphs are devoted to Mr. Glascock, who is connected to Nora Rowley as a possible suitor. His introduction among the guests at Lady Millborough's dinner party briefly interrupts the story of the Trevelyans' quarrel, and it allows Nora to appear in a new capacity, opening her up to still more connections. These are explored at much greater length in chapter 4, almost the whole of which is spent introducing Hugh Stanbury, Nora's other would-be suitor, and placing her in the familiar Trollopian position of suspension between two eligible men. Hugh's introduction, however, also includes brief descriptions of life at Nuncombe Putney and at Exeter, places where Hugh exists in other connections than his primary one to Nora. This second interruption of the Trevelyans' story—four times longer than the digression on Mr. Glascock in chapter 3—is concluded at the end of chapter 4, when Hugh meets Louis Trevelyan on the street. Chapters 5 and 6 concentrate on the Trevelyans again, but chapters 7 and 8 make another interruption, this one twice as long as its predecessor, dealing with the characters at Nuncombe Putney and Exeter who were introduced in chapter 4. Hugh is only a minor character in the lives of his sister and aunt. Once introduced, their stories go on to make a more or less independent "plot" of their own.

Nora Rowley, who starts out in the first two chapters as an apparently unimportant participant in the "main story" of the Trevelyans, becomes the principal means by which that story attains its "full development." Her relation to Hugh Stanbury motivates the introduction of the characters at Exeter and Nuncombe Putney; her relation to Mr. Glascock leads to the introduction of the Spaldings and the American and British community at Florence. At the far limit in one direction are Mr. Gibson and the French sisters, who never meet and barely hear of Louis Trevelyan. At the far limit in the other direction is Wallachia Petrie, "the Republican Browning," who also knows of Trevelyan only by hearsay. None of these characters, however, is more than three removes from Trevelyan by way of Nora Rowley. The Frenches are introduced in completion of Mr. Gibson, who completes Dorothy Stanbury, who in turn completes her brother Hugh. Wallachia Petrie completes Caroline Spalding, who completes Mr. Glascock. As each new set of characters is introduced, the "interruptions" in the story of Trevelyan's madness grow steadily longer, reaching a peak at the approximate center of the novel, where for a space of fourteen chapters (45 to 58) Trevelyan does not appear at all.

One can easily imagine that this domino narrative, which introduces more and more new characters in order to round out those who have gone before, might lead, if not controlled, to an endlessly expanding novel, which would not even have the real-life limit of the world's finite population to halt its growth. This is the threat of interminable writing, at once the nightmare and the fuel of the novel-machine. But as *He Knew He Was Right* expands, it provides insurance that it will eventually end. This insurance is the course of Trevelyan's madness, of which all expansions are supposed to be the "development." Trevelyan makes two mad journeys to Italy and back; all the subordinate characters are introduced during the first journey and disposed of during the second. The Frenches first appear, briefly, in chapter 15. They are dealt with at greater length in chapters 25 and 44, and they are the principal subjects of chapter 47. Wallachia Petrie, the last important character to be introduced, arrives in chapters 55 and 56. After Trevelyan returns to London in chapter 59, the expanding novel begins to contract. The Frenches are prominent again in chapters 65, 74, and 83, after which they disappear from the novel until its conclusion. Wallachia Petrie appears again in chapters 76, 77, and 81, after which she becomes the first character to be dropped from the novel, as she had been the last to be picked up by it. Before chapter 59, characters are introduced in order of decreasing closeness to Louis Trevelyan. After chapter 59, they are disposed of in reverse order, until Louis and Emily are left alone in chapter 98, to conclude the quarrel they began in chapter 1.

He Knew He Was Right has a kind of symmetry, centered upon the chapters of Trevelyan's absence and governed by the rhythm of his two departures and two returns. For the most part, the stories of the other characters proceed independently of Trevelyan's, interrupting his progress in a pattern set up by the first few chapters and elaborated upon thereafter. The result is a leapfrogging narrative: as the chapters build a linear sequence of numbered units, the story line shifts from one plot to another, seldom allowing more than two consecutive chapters to deal with the continuous development of one set of characters. Each set of characters is also centered in a different place—Emily, Hugh, and Nora in London; Miss Stanbury, Mr. Gibson, and the French sisters at Exeter; Dorothy and her mother at Nuncombe Putney—so that a complex system of movement through space is superimposed on the straight-line arithmetic of the increasing chapter numbers. Though they all begin in a specific place, however, not all the groups of characters stay put. Many of them move about in a manner that establishes cross connections among plots that would otherwise only run parallel.

Through Hugh Stanbury's efforts, Emily and Nora are sent to stay with his mother and sister at Nuncombe Putney, where they remain between chapters 14 and 32. In this way, they are brought one degree closer to the situation at Exeter. Miss Stanbury, who never leaves Exeter, can now plausibly hear about the quarrel and have an opinion on Emily's behavior. Nora can also have an opinion about Dorothy Stanbury, who has gone to Exeter to live with her aunt. In an analogous way during the second half of the novel, Emily, Nora, and their parents travel to Florence, where they remain for the similar span of chapters 75 to 93. This time it is Nora's connection to Mr. Glascock that motivates the transfer; the Rowleys are introduced to the Spaldings, and another exchange of opinions is made. At this advanced stage of Trevelyan's decrepitude, Mr. Glascock takes on a mediating role much like Hugh Stanbury's in the first half of the novel, interrupting his own affairs to visit Casalunga, offering advice to Emily and Nora. The crucial triad of Hugh, Nora, and Mr. Glascock, which opens up the two directions of the novel's expansion, is also the principal device by which that expansion is limited. Again following the scheme of Trevelyan's departure and return, the highly movable Emily and Nora are brought into contact first with the Stanbury side and then with the Glascock side, guaranteeing that the end of the novel will come and that it will be connected to the beginning.

The spatiality of any narrative is figurative, whether that space be the representation of a surface or the conjunction of two "places" in the text itself. Trollope's theory treats character as a zone or space on a canvas, while it assigns to plot the qualities of linearity and temporality that belong to the act of writing. *He Knew He Was Right* contains a thoroughly consistent fictional chronology, running without a digression from the first page of the novel to the last. The total action of the novel takes place within about eighteen months of fictional time, and changes in the personnel of its chapters have no effect on the ticking of its fictional clock. The story line may leapfrog from Exeter to London and back, but whatever time has passed in London is found also to have passed in Exeter, though unnarrated, when the narrative returns there. The novel's first six chapters, for example, are occupied by the events from 3 May to 7 May. Chapters 7 and 8, the first devoted to Miss Stanbury and Exeter, pick her up at some time in late April and narrate her activities until an unspecified day after May 7. Chapters 9 through 11 return to the Trevelyans, picking them up "one Sunday morning when the month of May was nearly over" and following them until Wednesday, 1 June. Chapter 12 returns to Exeter, rejoining Miss Stanbury "one Wednesday morning early in June." These twelve chapters consume about a month, although the Trevelyans are absent for all but the first and last days of it and Miss Stanbury for at least a week in the latter part of May.

Nevertheless, time has passed for London and Exeter equally, no matter whether London, Exeter, or nothing at all has occupied that time.

The *Autobiography* advises the would-be novelist to pay special attention to the changes that come with time, because such changes are especially "realistic": "And as, here in our outer world, we know that men and women change,—become worse or better as temptation or conscience may guide them,—so should these creations of his change, and every change should be noted by him. On the last day of each month recorded, every person in his novel should be a month older than on the first" (200). It has been generally recognized that this concern with gradual change is a distinctive feature of Trollope's fiction. As R. H. Hutton remarked in 1867, Trollope's power "is not intensive and concentrated, but extensive and gradual in its approaches." His novels provide "view after view of his different characters, each looking, at first, as if it were only the old view over again, but proving before long to have a something added, which gives a sense of completer knowledge of the character."[20] A large canvas, as Hutton also notes, is necessary to this method: Trollope is at his most Trollopian when he works with a large number of characters and a multitude of words. The double structure of *He Knew He Was Right*—a leapfrogging narrative combined with a linear chronology —illustrates how this special Trollopian effect is produced. The sense of gradual change derives from the rhythmical departure and return of the characters. Very little of their development is narrated at any one time; most of the chapters are directly concerned with the activities of no more than a day or two. But the novel offers a long string of such brief scenes, separated from each other by interludes of several days or weeks during which other characters in other places are described. Every time a character returns from absence—and almost every chapter in the novel brings such a return—he is found to be not quite the same as he was at his last appearance. The character has been living and changing while the narrative was busy elsewhere, and now it is the business of the narrative to record the effects of what happened during that unnarrated but nevertheless real time.

One result of this method is that, though the sense of gradually changing characters is Trollope's forte, change is hardly ever explicitly stated. Only twice in *He Knew He Was Right* is a character said to have changed. Miss Stanbury is "very much altered from the Miss Stanbury of old" (89), and Dorothy's "character" has "changed, as does that of a

[20]Review of *Lotta Schmidt and Other Stories, Spectator* 40 (21 September 1867): 1062.

flower when it opens itself in its growth" (97). Both of these comments come late in the novel, and neither is elaborated upon. Though change is constantly in progress among all the characters, the reader is almost always left on his own to identify it. Change takes place while the characters are outside the narrative, and the discovery of change happens in the reader's mind—his own supplement to a text that does not state its meaning. The text only leaves room for meaning; the reader must imagine what that space contains. Trollope's distinctive narrative method is the (necessarily) tacit assertion that the reality of the text is never in the text but on both sides of it—in the world of the characters, where life goes on at an equal pace whether or not it is written down, and in the world of the reader, where unwritten life is imagined to have taken place. That unwritten life is allowed for by the multiple gaps that open between the straight line of time and the zigzag of the narrative. The most important things in Trollope's fiction are the differences between this time and the last time, differences that can only be explained by the unwritten life that has been going on continuously from then to now.

The chronology of *He Knew He Was Right* is also, like plot in the theory, a figure for writing. Fictional time passes in pace with the watch that ticks on the novelist's writing desk and assures his production of 250 words every fifteen minutes. Fictional time passes equally no matter what is being narrated, just as writing goes on steadily no matter what is being written. Time is a figure for the text, for its sequence of words, pages, and chapters. It is a figure for the reader's experience of the text, the progress he makes from one page or chapter to the next in numbered sequence. Time is not, however, a figure for the reader's experience of character. That is figured by the zigzagging narrative line, which moves from place to place on a fictional surface, sketching character as it goes. That surface is the surface of the represented world, the places where characters are said to be and where, as I shall show, they act themselves out spatially. But it is also the textual space constituted in imagination by the simultaneity of multiple plots. The text cannot directly portray simultaneity, nor does it often attempt to do so by such phrases as "meanwhile" or "at the same time." Instead, the interaction of continuous time with discontinuous narration persuades the reader, each time he begins a chapter, to connect its characters with the last time he read about them, which could have been as few as two or as many as fifteen chapters earlier. Time has gone forward regularly. The unwritten life of these characters must have been happening at the same time as the written life of those other characters whose stories have intervened, though it is seldom said to have done so. When this technique is amplified to five or six plots, each interrupting and interrupted by the others, and when the separate plots are also distinguished as separate movements from place to place, the result is an imaginary surface created by the multiplication of imaginary time. It is on this imaginary surface that character is inscribed.

The hackneyed figures of plot as a thread and character as a portrait, which Trollope adopts wholeheartedly from common wisdom, describe his own narrative practice rather well. Both of them, as I have shown, are figures for writing in Trollope's theory, and in his novels they cannot exist otherwise than as written. But the discontinuity of the individual plots, combined with the continuity of a single calendar governing the whole novel, requires an imaginative effort to bring separated chapters together, thereby employing the linearity of writing to construct an imagined spatial unity. This unity, like the intervening life that remains unwritten, is not stated in the text. The reader is persuaded to construct the surface for himself; the gaps in the written text are rhetorical devices, persuading the reader to imagine a space that the text cannot represent. Even the gaps are figurative; the text of *He Knew He Was Right*, like its calendar, is continuous from first page to last. But the characters are interrupted, and these interruptions, signs of the inability of writing to be in two places at once, require that the failure of writing be repaired by unwritten sympathy. Writing thereby performs just what Trollope's theory says it should—its own effacement. A typical case will show how this feat is performed.

In chapter 11 of *He Knew He Was Right*, Louis Trevelyan writes a letter to his wife and dates it Wednesday, 1 June. The rest of the chapter takes place on the afternoon and evening of the same day. Chapter 12 begins "on one Wednesday morning early in June," a day that might be 1 June but is not specified as such. Nor is it specified as the day on which Trevelyan wrote his letter. In this case as in all others, the times of the separate plots are not cross referenced; the novel's uniform calendar is the reference for all the plots, and no plot takes direct cognizance of its interruption by any other. Chapter 12 is also typical in that, having made at its start a fairly precise designation of time, it harks back:

> On one Wednesday morning early in June, great preparations were being made at the brick house in the Close at Exeter. . . . Mrs. Stanbury and her elder daughter were coming into Exeter from Nuncombe Putney to visit Dorothy. The reader may perhaps remember that when Miss Stanbury's

invitation was sent to her niece, she was pleased to promise that such visits
should be permitted on a Wednesday morning. Such a visit was now to be
made. . . .

The promise recalled here was made in a similar retrospective passage at
the start of chapter 8, the last chapter in which Exeter has appeared. The
reader is prompted to link chapters 8 and 12 in a continuous action, but
not to omit the time (about two weeks) that has passed in the three
intervening chapters. The beginning of chapter 12 not only establishes
the continuity of the plot centered in Exeter but it also includes in that
continuity the interruption of London. At the start of chapter 12,
Trevelyan becomes a part of Miss Stanbury's past.

Later in the introductory paragraph, a conversation is introduced
that took place "on the afternoon of the preceding day"—that is, Tuesday,
the day before the "beginning" of the chapter. For about a page, Miss
Stanbury discusses with her servant Martha her nervous anticipation of
the guests' arrival. The narrative then returns to its starting point, again
harks back briefly, and settles into another conversation, which leads to
the expected event:

> But when the morning came Miss Stanbury was still in a twitter. Half-past
> ten had been the hour fixed for the visit, in consequence of there being a train
> in from Lessboro', due at the Exeter station at ten. As Miss Stanbury
> breakfasted always at half-past eight, there was no need of hurry on account
> of the expected visit. But, nevertheless, she was in a fuss all the morning; and
> spoke of the coming period as one in which she must necessarily put herself
> into solitary confinement.

In its manipulation of time, this commonplace two-page introduction is
as subtle as it is typical of Trollope's unobtrusive craft. The title of the
chapter, "Miss Stanbury's Generosity," anticipates what is to come. Then
a date is provided that puts the chapter in place according to the novel's
calendar and coordinates it indirectly with the chapter that has just
ended. Next, the narrative recalls its last visit to Exeter, connecting
chapters 8 and 12 without omitting the time between. Then it repeats this
back-and-forth movement on a smaller scale, returning to Wednesday
morning, recalling the previous afternoon, and coming back once more
to the state of anticipation with which it began. This smooth manipulation
of three narrative tenses sets up a zone of time in which the main action
of the chapter is carried out. Then, at its end, the chapter links itself
backward and forward in a similar manner—announcing an advance to
"the next morning," recalling Miss Stanbury's earlier behavior, and
concluding in anticipation of a move to be made two months in the

future. The chapter ends as it began, merged with what precedes and follows it in an ongoing process of memory and anticipation.

Trollope's calendar for *He Knew He Was Right* is both vague and precise. Notations of date rarely give both the day of the week and its number in the month, and the year is never more precise than "186-." Events are most commonly located, as in the case of chapter 12, by reference to preceding events and those to come. Sometimes, however, there is no reference to the novel's calendar, so that events cannot be placed more precisely than somewhere between earlier and later events. In a few cases, the introductory sentence advances the narrative a month or more, and the whole chapter is taken up by a retrospective summary of what has happened during that period, returning only at the end of the chapter to the time named at its start. In one case, chapter 13, the initial time is not regained until the middle of the following chapter. Some anticipated events link several chapters together. Sir Marmaduke Rowley's arrival, for example, is looked forward to from chapter 5, when it is first decided upon, until chapter 61, when he finally arrives. His departure, the date of which is fixed in chapter 85, serves to measure the passage of time until chapter 94, when it occurs. These characteristic Trollopian techniques, different as they are, all involve a constant alternation of looking back and looking forward. The result is that, as time advances in pace with the novel's advancing page count, the reader is persuaded to subvert its progress by regarding each chapter not as a way station or a link in a chain but as a zone that merges with what precedes and follows it. No scene or chapter stands fully apart from the rest, and no one event makes a standard for all the others. Rather, when these techniques are multiplied on the grand scale of this very long novel, when each chapter is merged with at least two others and they in turn with more, time is spread out, and an imaginary space is constituted by multiplied time.

This is the characteristic Trollopian method of novel construction, exhibited at its most elaborate in *He Knew He Was Right* but visible at varying degrees of extension in his other novels as well. The method achieves its most complex effects when several plots are in progress; Gordon Ray is correct, for this reason and others, in claiming that one ought to pay most attention to Trollope's "big books," because his "major energies throughout his career" were devoted to them.[21] But these big books are not, therefore, Trollope's most meaningful or even most elegant. In itself, the method makes no guarantee that the various plots that it so

[21] "Trollope at Full Length," p. 319.

handily combines will be related in any other way. Still less does it assure
that the entire novel will converge on a single lesson or that it will be
unified thematically. The *Autobiography* stresses that a novel, no matter
how big it is, must be "all one," and that there should be no "episodes"
like the story of the Man of the Hill in *Tom Jones*, because such impertinent matters "distract the attention of the reader, and always do so
disagreeably" (204). Trollope's characteristic method, however, is capable
of linking any number of otherwise disparate plots together and making
them "all one." So long as the plots are simultaneous, so long as their
presence in the same novel is motivated by the expedients of familial or
romantic relations, the method requires no further likeness among the
plots to weld them into a unified whole. It is not even able to end a novel,
or to start one. One reason why, as I have shown in chapter 6, the beginnings and endings of Trollope's novels are points of particular arti-
ficiality is that his fundamental method of construction is one of
continuation, not of starting or stopping. Time, plot, and writing itself
share this potential for infinite forward movement. They all require the
imposition of limits, coming from outside themselves, to make them
conform to any dimensions. These limits take numerous forms—from the
timetable made up in advance and strictly observed to the prearranged
number of installments or volumes to be filled to the symmetrical introduction and dismissal of characters that I have discussed above—but the
most important of them is character, the inscription on the imaginary
surface that makes writing stop by binding it to the real, unwritten
world.

　　Trollope's theory treats character as an area of surface, and it is the
enclosure of this area, the fact that it has limits all round, that saves the
realistic novelist from the endless exaggerations of writing for its own
sake. In *He Knew He Was Right*, characters are introduced in association
with some real-life place, and their subsequent movements from that
place to others sketch out a pattern of action that is as "characteristic" of
them as their names. The surface on which they move is the surface of the
real world; the figures that they trace there are their own reality. The
imaginary surface of the narrative coincides with the represented solid
earth on which, according to the *Autobiography*, all realistic characters
stand, and which becomes in Hawthorne's metaphor a figure for the
whole realistic enterprise. In the first six chapters of *He Knew He Was
Right*, for example, the characters of Louis and Emily Trevelyan, Nora
Rowley, and Colonel Osborne are set in distinctive kinds of motion to
which they will adhere, on whatever greater or smaller scale, throughout

the novel. Each of them establishes a habit of going and coming, meeting and avoiding other characters, remaining present or becoming absent, that literally de-fines him and that can be expanded or contracted to any dimension of space or pages. Emily begins in separation from her husband, confiding to her patient sister the nature of their quarrel. She then receives Colonel Osborne in private, confides in Nora again, and waits for her husband to come to her, though this time he does not. In chapter 3, she accompanies Louis to Lady Millborough's party, but they do not confront each other again until the end of the evening. In chapters 4 and 5, she again does not see her husband; but in chapter 6, through Nora's inter-vention, an equivocal reconciliation is made, after which husband and wife take a walk and again meet Colonel Osborne.

Emily's case is far from the most complex or interesting in *He Knew He Was Right*, but it is typical. From the first, she goes where she is told to go and stays there until someone tells her to move on. She sits in her room waiting to be sent for or visited; she receives communications of any sort from any quarter, but she initiates nothing. Her "character," as she sketches it within the narrow confines of her own house, is a stubborn tendency to stay where she is and submit to pressure. She shares with most of the characters in this novel, and with a great number of Trollope's other characters, an obstinate devotion to her own characteristic pattern of movement, though in her case the devotion amounts to a paradoxical refusal not to respond to any push that comes her way. She is a sort of parody of the dutiful, submissive wife, whose only option is to obey and who resists by refusing not to surrender.[22] But she is also a rhythm of reception, obedience, going with, and being sent. Like the other characters in *He Knew He Was Right*, she repeats this rhythm over and over again, across ever broader stretches of time and space. She acts herself out twice within the first two chapters in her home, then twice again within the next four chapters at Lady Millborough's and in Kensington Gardens. Eighteen chapters then take her obediently to Nuncombe Putney, and two great blocks of about thirty chapters each carry her to St. Diddulph's, Florence, Casalunga, and back again to England—all the time waiting for orders and obeying them, just as she does in chapter 1.

The geography of *He Knew He Was Right* is more complex and far ranging than that of Trollope's other novels, and the connection between character and movement across a surface is therefore more prominent here than is usually the case. Yet even in *He Knew He Was Right*, where

---

[22]The roles of women in this novel and in *The Vicar of Bullhampton* are sensitively analyzed by Ruth apRoberts in "Emily and Nora."

characters travel thousands of miles in their self-enactment, they begin by tracing themselves within the confined spaces of houses or cities. The pattern, like the amplification of any novel to fit its "canvas," retains its shape no matter what its size becomes. No Victorian novelist made more thorough use of the map of England than Trollope did; his characters borrow their natures from their addresses, and they act those natures out in journeys from one address to another. On an even smaller scale than this, the characters in all Trollope's novels establish patterns of arrival, departure, joining, and separating that are more than mechanisms for making scenes. They are the characters, figures drawn on a surface made of time. Not all the characters in *He Knew He Was Right* are as mobile as the Trevelyans; Miss Stanbury, for example, never leaves Exeter and hardly ever goes out from the aptly named "Close." But she is known by those who come to her, and her character is made up of an alternating series of rejections and acceptances. Her first action in the novel is the pseudoadoption of her niece Dorothy. Later she sends Dorothy away, only to ask her back again. She does the same with her nephew Hugh, shutting him out at first, then welcoming him, and with Mr. Gibson, allying herself with him and then excluding him from her favor. The alignments that characters make or break are spatial as well as characteristic; they define zones of operation that are not only the range or scope of character, they are character itself.

In general, however, the characters of *He Knew He Was Right* are on the move with great frequency and over great distances. Dorothy goes from Nuncombe Putney to Exeter; Mr. Glascock goes from London to Nuncombe Putney to Florence to Naples; the Spaldings come from America to Florence; the elder Rowleys come from the Mandarin Islands and return there; Nora and Emily travel through almost all these places. Characters are defined by where they come from and where they are able to go. At the farthest distance from Louis Trevelyan, movement is comically restricted, while for him it is tragically boundless. The French sisters, despite their names, are literally unable to get out of Exeter; and Wallachia Petrie, despite hers, enacts America in the heart of Florence. Between these extremes, characters face decisions of love and loyalty that are also decisions of movement. Nora must choose between poverty in London and splendor at Monkhams. Dorothy has the choice of penury at Nuncombe Putney or comfortable bondage at Exeter. Caroline Spalding chooses England over America. Whether it is projected into the future as desire or enacted in the present as transportation, repeated movement in a distinctive pattern defines character.

This definition does not permit the acquisition of new characteristics during the course of the novel. Each character has at his introduction all the traits or patterns of movement that he will ever have. "Change," important as it is to the Trollopian novel, amounts only to the acting out of various capabilities at various times, or the enactment of some capabilities and the suppression of others. Very often, the choice of how to be corresponds to the choice of where to go or whom to marry; Trollope's characters vacillate between conflicting aspects of their natures according to the same figuratively spatial patterns that govern the choice of homes or husbands. In *He Knew He Was Right*, Nora, Caroline Spalding, and both French sisters consider choices of love that are also choices of residence. But Miss Stanbury, who is beyond marriage or desire to leave home, vacillates just as rhythmically between obstinacy and acquiescence. Both characteristics are established early in the novel. She enters the narrative with a history of obstinate behavior, having refused friendship to the Burgesses and her nephew, but her first action in the novel is the adoption of her niece. Her alternation of affection and rejection is at the same time a spatial figure and a slow change of character. At the end she is certainly different from what she was at the start, but she has acquired nothing new. She has merely let her old generosity take precedence where once it was suppressed. The same is true, on a smaller scale, of Dorothy. Most of the time she is humbly submissive, but she shows an occasional flicker of the "Stanbury perversity" (36), and her ultimate assertion of self-will is only the enactment of what had always lain dormant in her. The time of plot, as Trollope's theory claims, adds nothing to the space of character. Plot only gives character a chance to sketch itself.

All these fundamental structures of the Trollopian novel are metonymic, in that they depend on relations of juxtaposition rather than the substitutions of metaphor. The leapfrogging of plots, the repetitive performance of character, the steady advance of fictional time—all contribute to the construction of a figurative surface where meaning is movement and comparison. Metonymy is as well the governing figure of Trollope's theory, which places novelist and characters, reader and fiction, fiction and reality, side by side. Hawthorne's figure of a world under glass —though the figure itself is a metaphor, and so the very opposite of what Trollope would have invented—makes the whole Trollopian project a vast metonymy, where the reader comes face to face with an enclosed chunk of the same earth he stands on. Trollope would therefore be, according to Jakobson's famous scheme, the most realistic of novelists, opposed to the metaphors of romanticism and symbolism alike. But Trollope's realism also includes an interdict against all figuration, the insistence that what realistic metonymy constructs is not a system of signification—though, to an observer, both his theory and his practice are exactly that. Hawthorne's metaphor also accommodates this feature of Trollopian realism: the glass of the text is as little *there* as possible, a thing to be looked through rather than looked at; but it is undeniably there, the transparent imperfection that guarantees that the metonymy of reality and fiction will never be perfect because a tiny metaphoric leap must always be made.

I began this chapter by making a case for the privileged position of *He Knew He Was Right* among Trollope's forty-seven novels, but so far I have treated it (synecdochically) as typical. It is in keeping with Trollope's theory that all the products of the novel-machine should be much like each other, contiguous sections of the continuous real earth. But I have been able to treat *He Knew He Was Right* as a typical Trollopian product only by postponing discussion of the one thing that makes it extraordinary: the character of Louis Trevelyan, Trollope's unique full-length portrait of madness, the one aspect of the novel that makes it decidedly different from all Trollope's others. Trevelyan is responsible for the pervading sombre tone of the novel, which many mid-Victorian critics found distasteful. He is also responsible for the highest praise the novel ever received, Henry James's comment in his "Partial Portrait" that the scene of Trevelyan at Casalunga is "worthy of Balzac."[23] And he is, most significantly, the reason for Trollope's own judgment, in the *Autobiography*, that *He Knew He Was Right* is "almost altogether bad": "It was my purpose to create sympathy for the unfortunate man who, while endeavouring to do his duty to all around him, should be led constantly astray by his unwillingness to submit his own judgment to the opinion of others. The man is made to be unfortunate enough, and the evil which he does is apparent. So far I did not fail, but the sympathy has not been created yet" (276). Sympathy is the sole aim of realistic writing and the sole pleasure and profit of reading any novel; to fail at this is to fail totally. Trollope never damned any of his other novels so absolutely, and again Louis Trevelyan is responsible.

According to the *Autobiography*, Trevelyan's story is the "main part" of *He Knew He Was Right*, to which everything else is "subordinate." The operation of the novel, as I have discussed it above, includes no three-dimensional provision for subordination. All the plots leapfrog on

[23] *Critical Heritage*, p. 543.

the same ground, and all the characters are painted on the same canvas. The distinction of main and subordinate parts has, like character, a limiting function. It assures that the novel will have a beginning, an end, and an attachment to the real world. Like Trollope's other novels, *He Knew He Was Right* names its "main part" in its title—though in this case the naming is somewhat shifty, since it depends on the precedence of a pronoun over its antecedent. But the novel begins with Louis Trevelyan, and it ends with him. Trevelyan and his immediate surroundings are also the starting place of the novel's expansion; they are the site of departure for all the other plots, which spread metonymically out from there. Trevelyan is not the "center" of the novel—neither Trollope's theory nor his practice allows for a sovereign point that could be called a center—nor does the novel devote significantly more pages to his adventures than to those of such subordinate characters as Nora, Hugh, and Miss Stanbury. But the repeatedly interrupted story of Louis Trevelyan provides a theme on which the rest of the plots are variations; his career makes a line rather than a point of reference for everything else in the novel. At least, these are the limiting functions that, according to the principle of "proportion," Louis Trevelyan's story ought to perform. Yet the cause of the novel's failure is the extraordinary conception of his story as one without limits, his figure as one without boundaries, his line as the endless self-advancement of writing itself.

In the early chapters of the novel, Trevelyan acts out his character much as Emily and Nora act out theirs. But there is a difference. They repeat themselves: Emily waits for Louis, Nora listens; Emily waits for Colonel Osborne, Nora listens again. Louis, however, though he has confronted his wife one time, refuses to do so again. Instead, when Colonel Osborne comes to visit, Louis stays downstairs, taking the sound of arriving and departing footsteps as a report of what is going on elsewhere in the house. Later, after Osborne has gone, Louis again avoids meeting his wife. He goes to his club, where he hears from a virtual stranger the "secret" that Emily and the colonel have been keeping from him. It is an innocent secret (they are plotting to get Emily's father transferred back to England from the remote and sweltering Mandarins), and its secrecy has the odd characteristic of having been created by the man from whom the secret is kept: "Hitherto, indeed, his wife, as the reader knows, could not have told him. He had not seen her since the matter had been discussed between her and her friend. But he was angry because he first learned at his club that which he thought he ought to have learned at home" (3). Louis has already made two substitutions for the direct confrontation with his wife that he dared to have once, before the novel began. First he prefers the sound of footsteps to the people who produce it. Then he listens to the gossip of a casual acquaintance rather than to the testimony of the woman who, characteristically, would tell him everything if he would only ask. He once had immediate contact with Emily, but he has exchanged it for the space of a flight of stairs, then for a few city blocks. Already he is himself, and like Trollope's characters in general, he will never be anything else. But the figure of his character does not close itself off. Instead it opens gaps that slowly widen. The gaps are spatial—a few feet, a mile—and also temporal, because the Louis Trevelyan of one moment is unable to recognize the arrangements made by the Louis Trevelyan of another.

Face-to-face contact is the scene of Trollopian community. Character can state itself fully, and sympathy can be fully achieved, only when proximity allows signification to be replaced by metonymic equivalence. Louis Trevelyan's character is unique in Trollope because its enactment precludes its statement. His character enacts itself in the typical Trollopian way, by gradual amplification of its given figure, but that figure is eccentric, unable to return to where it began. Louis at the Acrobats Club (an appropriate name) is not the same man who chose to go there, just as Louis in his study can resent his wife's absence as if it were someone else, and not Louis himself a few hours before, who told her to go away. Character can be stated only when the speaker and the listener are one, inside each mind and between minds. But it is, paradoxically, the statement of Louis Trevelyan's character that the speaker and the listener are always different and become more so. Louis is always an oblique step away from where he last found himself; looking back, he is unable to establish the identity of here and there. The very conception of his character makes sympathy impossible, because no one can get close enough to him to read him. And the enactment of that character is a parody of Trollopian reading or its nightmare, because instead of looking back and recognizing his continuity with what he was, linking himself to himself as the reader of a Trollopian novel ought to do, Louis always insists on a difference, generating out of his present a crowd of past Louises on which the death of the generator is the only limit.

Each time Louis reenacts himself, the scope of his off-centeredness grows. From his club he moves to the Full Moon public house, then to Paris (32); from there he goes over the Alps (33) to Turin (38). In chapter 59, he returns to London, but to a remote suburb and a house called

River's Cottage (67). Again he crosses the Alps into Italy, ending up at desolate Casalunga, which is, as those who seek him out there are told, not "on the way to any place" (78). From Casalunga Trevelyan makes ineffectual plans to travel to still more distant places, but by this time he has become so physically and mentally debilitated that he is unable to resist the pressure of his wife and friends, who carry him back through Italy and France to England, thereby completing the second transcontinental tracing out of his character. From his failure to appear at luncheon in chapter 1 and his refusal to speak to Emily in chapter 2, Trevelyan's enactment of separation and substitution grows monstrously into two grand passages across Europe and back, each of which traverses about forty chapters. But he remains true to himself from start to finish, moving with relentless consistency through stage after stage of physical and emotional distance from those who should be close to him.

At no time, however, does Trevelyan want absolute separation. It is the oddest feature of his character that the distances and distortions of its enactment are generated by the desire to make contact with those from whom that same desire is always driving him farther away. He wants contact, but he refuses or is unable to participate in the sign-free communication that holds the Trollopian community together. He insists on signs and symbols, thinking that they will bring him truth, but all they bring him are more signs and symbols, each a little falser than the last. Signs require interpretation; they permit error. The wordless mutual reading that constitutes Trollopian love is free from interpretation and therefore cannot be wrong. Nowhere in *He Knew He Was Right* is it explained why Trevelyan prefers signs to the thing signified; it is his built-in paradox that the truth of his character, which ought to be stated without language, consists in the inability to make such a statement. Nowhere in the novel is it explained why this insistence on interpretation rather than love should result in a madly insatiable desire to keep moving, over greater and greater distances, always farther away from the very thing he wants to know.

Trollope's theory, however, suggests an explanation. Trevelyan enacts the nightmare of the novel-machine; he gives himself without reserve to the boundless proliferation of signs that the whole mechanism of Trollope's theory is designed to contain and subjugate. It is as if his story were an experiment, an attempt to portray by means of the novel-machine the thing that threatens it most. For once, as Henry James remarks, Trollope has attempted in the character of Louis Trevelyan to be "thoroughly logical"; "he has not been afraid of a misery which should be too much like life."[24] Louis is not granted those magical moments of character statement that, supremely unlike life as they are, hold Trollope's fictional world together. He is, perhaps, all the more realistic for that reason. Yet the novel-machine, driven past its own limits, can find no end to Trevelyan's logic but madness and death.

On his way to death, Trevelyan passes through many stages of substitution. First he listens to footsteps, then to gossip. Then he takes to writing letters to his wife and sends Lady Millborough along with a letter as dual ambassadors who cancel each other out (5). As each new substitution fails to bring the satisfaction he desires, he perversely chooses a remoter medium, getting farther away in space and stretching the chain of signification still longer. He sends Emily into the wilds of Devonshire and puts himself into a second-rate London hotel. He exhausts the patience of his friends by making spies and couriers of them. And then, driven beyond the boundaries of acquaintance and class, he hires Bozzle, the detective, and brings the word "madness" into the novel for the first time (19). In one sense, Bozzle is a satire on the standard detective of sensation novels. Unlike those glamorous literary creatures, Bozzle has a wife and baby, and he always addresses Trevelyan as "Mr. Trewillian." Bozzle is another Trollopian correction of sensationalism, and contemporary critics recognized him as such.[25] But though Bozzle is a comic figure, his role in Tevelyan's degeneration is full of tragic overtones. His name echoes that of the treacherous Bosola in Webster's *Duchess of Malfi*, and he is likened to a modern-day Iago, to whom Trevelyan plays an enfeebled Othello (45). Trevelyan eventually drives himself beyond even Bozzle's influence, but while he suffers from it the novel makes one of Trollope's bitterest attacks on sensationalism and the madness of interpreting signs.

Bozzle's specialty is "facts," miscellaneous bits of information that may be given any pattern the interpreter desires. He is able to tell Trevelyan the exact times when Colonel Osborne entered and left the house at Nuncombe Putney—these are "facts"—but he has no idea what happened in between: "There is things, Mr. Trewillian, which one can't see." Bozzle is able to get no closer to the truth than Trevelyan was when he sat in his study and listened to footsteps on the stairs; his "facts," comments the narrator, are "odious details,—details not one of which possessed the slightest importance" (23). But Bozzle is able to interpret his facts very handily, filling in the gaps between them with the low deduc-

[24] Ibid.
[25] See the *Times* review, *Critical Heritage*, p. 331.

tions of his own policeman's experience. Trevelyan becomes, in Bozzle's interpretation, "any gentleman acting in our way" (23), and Emily is "a lady as likes her fancy-man" (45). Bozzle reads nothing but "broken vows, secrecy, intrigue, dirt, and adultery" in the facts he gathers (33); to read them, he need only "put too and too together, as I always does" (45).

This putting too together, this interpretation of "facts," as the narrator makes clear more than once, is nothing but a strategy to keep Bozzle himself in operation: "Men whose business it is to detect hidden and secret things are very apt to detect things which have never been done. What excuse can a detective make even to himself for his own existence if he can detect nothing?" (28). Like sensationalism, like poetry, like writing itself, Bozzle's interpretive efforts are their own excuse and their own reward. The sordid romance he constructs, as the reader of *He Knew He Was Right* is repeatedly informed, has nothing whatever to do with the realistic story that is taking place "in truth." It is Trevelyan's tragedy not that he believes Bozzle's fact-fictions (he never quite believes them, though he is driven to ask for more and more), but that his nature is defiled by such associations: "To what a depth of degradation had he not been reduced!" (23). His self-made compulsion to interpret has driven him from home, from friends, from country, and even from class. He has sunk to the level of a sensational reader, the very opposite of a realist.

The compulsion, however, carries him even beyond Bozzle. By the time he first arrives in Paris, Tevelyan has come to believe that "there was indeed no one left to him but Bozzle" (32), yet in kidnapping little Louey he goes too far for even the strong-stomached ex-policeman (75), and at Casalunga he has come to hate Bozzle more than Colonel Osborne (84). Bozzle takes his place within a consistent, self-generating chain of substitutions that leads from a missed luncheon to the kidnapping of his son, and finally to the neglect of that last, remotest link with his starting point. Louey, like Trollopian children in general, is a piece of furniture. The child can barely speak, and he has no "facts" to offer. Trevelyan turns him into a symbol of everything that used to be his own—a perfect because perfectly empty symbol, into which any meaning at all can be read. Such free-flying symbols are the stuff of poetry: in chapter 78—the scene that James thought worthy of Balzac—Trevelyan has come not only to act like a poet but to look like a Pre-Raphaelite:

> He wore an old red English dressing-gown, which came down to his feet, and a small braided Italian cap on his head. His beard had been allowed to grow, and he had neither collar nor cravat. His trousers were unbraced, and he

> shuffled in with a pair of slippers, which would hardly cling to his feet. He was paler and still thinner . . . and his eyes seemed to be larger, and shone almost with a brighter brilliancy.

Eventually, Trevelyan claims that he has "got beyond" his symbolic child and that he has (literally) "no tie anywhere" (92). But even this next-to-last stage of transformation, into an unbraced poet, is in keeping with Trevelyan's character: in the first paragraph of the novel it is said that he had published "a volume of poems" before he was twenty-four. The gap that Trevelyan characteristically opens between himself and his world, and between versions of himself at different times, is the gap that characterizes sensationalism, romance, and poetry. It is a steady metaphoric drive away from sympathy, preferring all kinds of signs and symbols to the wordless love of the silently speaking heart. To succumb to that drive, to leap into that gap, is the same for the novel-machine as for Louis Trevelyan: it is madness.

The question of Trevelyan's madness is, however, a surprisingly difficult one. Trollope's method of character portrayal, the expanding enactment of traits that are all present at the start, makes no provision for going mad, just as it makes none for falling in love. When Ayala discovers that she loves Jonathan Stubbs, she discovers at the same time that she has always loved him; that love is her character, and she must always have been what she is. In Trollope's one other extensive portrayal of madness, Robert Kennedy goes mad sometime between novels. He is apparently sane at the end of *Phineas Finn* but is found at the start of *Phineas Redux* to be already insane. In *He Knew He Was Right*—written, perhaps coincidentally, in the interval between Kennedy's sanity and madness—no such easy escape is available. The novel poses itself the question of how, and at what moment, Trevelyan goes mad, yet it is incapable of answering its own question. If Louis is what he has always been, then he must have been mad from the first page of the novel. If he is sane at one point and mad at another, then the novel must portray what no other Trollope novel portrays and what Trollope's method cannot accommodate—the acquisition of a new characteristic during the course of the novel. If Trevelyan does go mad at some determinable moment, a further paradox ensues. It is the figure of his character that he fails to recognize the continuity of his past and present, but always treats his own past arrangements as if some other person had made them. To call him mad at one moment, and to admit that at an earlier moment he was not, would be in the oddest possible way to confirm his sanity, by allowing that the difference he always finds is really there. *He Knew He*

Was Right is unable to break this double bind; it vacillates constantly between the desire to call him mad and the compulsion to postpone the calling.

The word "madness" first appears in the novel in chapter 19, when the narrator remarks that "in these days of his madness" Trevelyan took Bozzle into his employ. But it is not until chapter 32 that one of the novel's most subordinate characters, Mr. Outhouse, suggests that "the only possible excuse" for Trevelyan's wild behavior is "that he must be mad." Chapter 38 bears the apparently conclusive title "Verdict of the Jury—'Mad, My Lord,'" but the chapter offers only an inconclusive meditation on the subject:

> There is perhaps no great social question so imperfectly understood among us at the present day as that which refers to the line which divides sanity from insanity. That this man is sane and that other unfortunately mad we do know well enough. . . . We know that the sane man is responsible for what he does, and that the insane man is irresponsible; but we do not know,—we only guess wildly, at the state of mind of those, who now and then act like madmen, though no court or council of experts has declared them to be mad.

If Trevelyan had gone so far as to "fancy himself to be a teapot, or what not," then judgment would be easy. But at the worst his madness is topical. He is, "in truth, mad on the subject of his wife's alleged infidelity," an apparently decisive statement that, in truth, only begs the question. Later, Reverend Outhouse complains that "this wicked madman" has destroyed the peace of St. Diddulph's (41), and still later Emily declares, "In very truth I do believe that he is mad" (60). But though some of the characters are able to reach their own decisions, the narrator is at pains throughout the novel to transform the question from a simple matter of yes or no into a complex problem of evaluation. Trevelyan, "mad as he was," is still sane enough not to seek the aid of a shabby lawyer (52). Because he feels "truly and with a keen accuracy" all the pain he has caused those around him, "if he were mad, he was not all mad" (67). Even very late in the novel, the narrator will make only the roundabout admission that "they who declared him to be mad were justified in their declaration." Then he adds the qualification that, if Trevelyan is mad, the "deep, correct, continued, and energetic" thinking of which he is capable must be "quite compatible with madness" (84).

The Trollopian narrator is usually the dispenser of "truth," following the antisensational principle of complete honesty that the *Autobiography* stresses and the novels repeat. The narrator of *He Knew He Was Right* performs this function most of the time, reminding the reader that "his wife, as the reader knows, could not have told him" (3) or granting the reader information that the characters do not possess: "At this very moment Trevelyan was in the house, but they did not know it" (60). On the subject of Trevelyan's madness, however, the narrator provides no "truth." Indeed, in the last chapters of the novel, there is an increasing eagerness on the part of narrator and characters alike to dispose of the question without answering it. "What can one do at any time with a madman?" thinks Hugh Stanbury in exasperation (92); and the narrator, equally exasperated, gives up on analysis a few pages later: "But who can tell how busy and how troubled are the thoughts of a madman!" (93). As Trevelyan slides toward the last extremity of debilitation, his wife gives up on decisiveness: "a man might be in such a condition as to be neither mad nor sane;—not mad, so that all power over his own actions need be taken from him; nor sane, so that he must be held accountable for his words and thoughts" (96). Even the doctor who attends Trevelyan on his deathbed can offer no final verdict. "In one sense," he unhelpfully admits, "all misconduct is proof of insanity" (98). And the narrator grows almost hysterically indecisive at the last: "And then, though they had determined between themselves in spoken words never to regard him again as one who had been mad, in all their thoughts and actions toward him they treated him as though he were less responsible than an infant. And he was mad;—mad though every doctor in England had called him sane. Had he not been mad he must have been a fiend. . . ." (98). In chapter 98, Trevelyan is "acquitted," but chapter 99 begins with the abrupt announcement "At last the maniac was dead," an apparent conviction, and the only time the decisive word "maniac" is used in the entire novel.

There is no final verdict on Louis Trevelyan, only a nearly interminable hedging about a question that seems always on the verge of being answered yet never is. As the narrator claims late in the novel, "The misery of the insane more thoroughly excites our pity than any other suffering to which humanity is subject; but it is necessary that the madness should be acknowledged before the pity can be felt" (98). One may doubt that such acknowledgement is necessary; one certainly doubts that it is as difficult as this novel finds it. Yet in his own terms Trollope is right to call the novel a failure, because the madness is never quite acknowledged, and as a result the required sympathy for Louis Trevelyan "has not been created yet" (*Autobiography*, 276).

As I have said, however, it is a distortion of the specifically Trollopian structure of *He Knew He Was Right* to abstract one plot from it and draw a conclusion, even when that plot is the novel's "main part" and the conclusion is that no conclusions can be drawn. The cooperation of a leapfrogging narrative and an ongoing calendar assures that the novel will not fall apart into a collection of separate plots and subplots; the acts of memory and anticipation that link the chapters of each plot together also include whatever has interrupted those chapters, and the reader is led (though never explicitly instructed) to regard all the plots as related in more than adventitious ways. Trevelyan's story makes a line of reference for the others, but if the novel really is "all one," then it is a mistake to see Trevelyan's story as central and the others as peripheral or episodic. Trevelyan interrupts the other characters as much as they interrupt him, and every plot interrupts every other — they are all equal to that degree. As in the case of gradual change, which is portrayed everywhere yet hardly ever stated, Trollope's method persuades the reader to read what remains unwritten: some principle or cluster of principles, some theme or suite of themes, that runs through all the portraits and makes them one. Again, Trollope's organization of time and space does not provide for thematic unification. If there are themes, they have a limiting function. They are a way of making each novel different from the rest, of making sure that each novel, once begun, will end, and of binding the novel to the real world of which it is supposed to be a part. They are also another way of persuading the reader to look beyond the text, because the thematic unity of any Trollope novel is as imaginary as the real-life space in which the novel is acted out.

All the characters of *He Knew He Was Right* face choices, ranging from Trevelyan's choice of wrath or reconciliation to Mr. Gibson's choice between the indistinguishably unappealing French sisters. Trevelyan sets the pace by a consistent choice of wrath, acted out in his characteristic pattern of absence and substitution. In the first chapters of the novel, each of his absences is accompanied by a reminder that an alternative has been abandoned. He fails to appear at luncheon, but "it would probably have been well that he should have done so now" (1). He listens to Colonel Osborne's footsteps and refuses to leave the drawing room, but "it would perhaps have been well had he done so" (2). When Osborne is gone, Trevelyan sets out for his club, but "had he gone to her now and said a word to her in gentleness all might have been made right. But he did not go to her" (2). After chapter 2, these nudges cease, and Trevelyan continues to make the same choice over and over again. But reconciliation is always an alternative, and the road untaken by Trevelyan remains open for all the other characters.

Chapters 7 and 8 introduce Miss Stanbury, who has "never spoken a word" to her brother's family since his death, and whose past therefore contains a choice of wrath like Trevelyan's. But by taking in her niece she is making one of the choices that Trevelyan has denied; her character is inconsistent, vacillating, and that much richer than Trevelyan's barren sameness. In chapter 10, Trevelyan's intensifying wrath brings the announcement to his wife, "Then we must part." Two chapters later, Miss Stanbury veers to her Trevelyan side, announcing to Dorothy, "you and I had better part" (12). Almost immediately, however, she relents, turning her partial resemblance to Trevelyan into a full contrast. Later, Miss Stanbury's "wrath" and her final break with Mr. Gibson (36 and 43) frame Trevelyan's arrival at the limit of his first outward journey (37 and 38). Her expulsion of Dorothy, which turns into reconciliation (57, 58, 66, 72, and 73), alternates in the narrative with the futile negotiations over Trevelyan's kidnapping of his son (61-65, 67, and 68). Dorothy returns to Exeter in chapter 73; the Rowleys pursue Trevelyan across the Alps in chapter 75. Throughout the novel, Miss Stanbury always comes before or after Trevelyan, and at both his extremes she diverges, taking the choice he leaves open, choosing reconciliation when he seeks only further estrangement.

If Miss Stanbury is in some ways a rectified Louis Trevelyan, one might be tempted to extend the analogy by looking for similarities between Dorothy, the principal object of her wrath, and Emily, the principal object of his. A series of juxtapositions encourages the extension. Emily decides to leave Nuncombe Putney in chapter 29, and Dorothy resolves to return there, if necessary, in chapter 30. Dorothy goes back to Exeter in chapter 73, and Emily goes to Italy in chapter 75. But Dorothy and Emily diverge just as Trevelyan and Miss Stanbury do. As Emily's obstinacy gradually softens, Dorothy's grows firmer, until in chapter 93 Emily at last begs forgiveness, and in chapter 98 Dorothy marries the man whose love Miss Stanbury has always forbidden her. Starting out in analogous positions, Dorothy and Emily end as opposites, and their careers, if one seeks to abstract a lesson from them, contradict each other. The pattern is made more complex by the addition of Nora, whom the narrative frequently places in juxtaposition to both Emily and Dorothy. Twice she refuses Mr. Glascock, the suitor of whom her family approves (13 and 17), and Dorothy twice spurns Mr. Gibson, whom her aunt has chosen to be her husband (36 and 43). Nora eventually marries Hugh, the forbidden lover, just as Dorothy marries the outcast Brooke Burgess. But on the way to happiness Nora encounters such stubborn resistance that she picks up an odd resemblance to Trevelyan himself, whose devotion to a single choice is no less obstinate than hers. In chapter 88, Nora is driven to contemplate running away from home in order to have her way. Later, she even faces the prospect of having no home at all (91), a prospect that opens up just one chapter before Trevelyan's triumphant announcement that he now has "no tie anywhere" (92). Dorothy and Nora come to resemble, at one point or another, both Trevelyan and his wife; yet the resemblance is always shifty. One can never make a simple equation or a simple negation. The four characters are repeatedly juxtaposed, and a great number of comparisons are possible; but any conclusion that might be drawn from the career of one character will be qualified out of existence by the careers of the other three.

When this scheme of multiplied partial resemblances is applied on the grand scale of *He Knew He Was Right*, it turns out that every character is in some way like and unlike every other, and some odd parallels indeed are produced. After Trevelyan is settled at Casalunga, for example, the farthest he will ever go, madness spreads among the other characters. Camilla French becomes as insane about her trousseau as Trevelyan is about his son, and she even vaguely echoes King Lear—"There never was anybody so badly treated,—never,—never,—never!" (82)—as Trevelyan will later do—"What's the news? Who's alive? Who dead? Who in? Who out?" (92). In the meantime, Mr. Gibson has decided that he was "quite demented" when he proposed to Camilla in the first place (82), and the unpleasant situation drives him to consider a Trevelyanish escape to "New Zealand,—or death" (83). And Lady Rowley, who suffers for a while from the delusion that Mr. Glascock is engaged to marry Wallachia Petrie, decides that both he and Nora must be insane (80). Parallels multiply till there is no choosing among them. The self-righteous obstinacy of the novel's title, which refers most obviously to Trevelyan, is displayed at one time or another by Emily (1), Miss Stanbury (12), Priscilla Stanbury (16), Nora (17), Hugh (21), Lady Millborough (33), Barty Burgess (35), Dorothy (42), Camilla French (65), and Caroline Spalding (81). Each of them knows he is right at some time and under some circumstances; the novel is full of obstinacy in an array of forms and situations. The characters are juxtaposed in as many permutations as they are capable of, and they generate such a multitude of similarities and differences that one is prevented from deciding, no matter how much one desires to decide, what is right and what is wrong.

Indeed, the best one can do in the way of a lesson from *He Knew He Was Right* is to say that the novel is "about" self-will and generosity, and their interaction. These two terms are the highest level of imaginative abstraction to which the novel can be raised, yet by the time one gets to that level one has left the novel so far behind that interpretation rests where Trollope's theory puts it—nowhere. Self-will and generosity make a moral economy that, like the literary economy of Trollope's theory, arrives at no synthesis. If there were a synthesis, it could be taken as the lesson that, according to Trollope, all novels are supposed to teach. But *He Knew He Was Right* teaches no lesson, and every aspect of its structure obstructs the effort to draw a moral from it. In one sense, however, *He Knew He Was Right* teaches, by example, the same lesson taught by all of Trollope's other novels and by his theory: that it is better to love than to interpret. There is no clearer case in Trollope's fiction of the madness that interpretation brings. But this lesson is a dream, dreamt by a man who could not, for the life of him, stop writing.

INDEX

The Johns Hopkins University Press

This book was set in Alphatype Palatino by David Lorton based on a design by Charles West. It was printed on 50-lb. Bookmark Natural Text paper and bound by Thomson-Shore, Inc.

Library of Congress Cataloging in Publication Data
Kendrick, Walter M
   The novel-machine.

   Includes bibliographical references and index.
   1. Trollope, Anthony, 1815-1882—Criticism and
interpretation. 2. Realism in literature. I. Title.
PR5687.K4   823'.8   79-18294
ISBN 0-8018-2301-3